Cazenovia

Past and Present
(Madison County, New York)

A DESCRIPTIVE AND HISTORICAL
RECORD OF THE VILLAGE

Christine O. Atwell

HERITAGE BOOKS
2012

HERITAGE BOOKS
AN IMPRINT OF HERITAGE BOOKS, INC.

Books, CDs, and more—Worldwide

For our listing of thousands of titles see our website
at
www.HeritageBooks.com

A Facsimile Reprint
Published 2012 by
HERITAGE BOOKS, INC.
Publishing Division
100 Railroad Ave. #104
Westminster, Maryland 21157

Entered according to the Act of Congress in the office of the
Librarian of Congress, A.D., 1928
by Christine O. Atwell
Cazenovia, New York

— Publisher's Notice —
In reprints such as this, it is often not possible to remove blemishes from the original. We feel the contents of this book warrant its reissue despite these blemishes and hope you will agree and read it with pleasure.

International Standard Book Numbers
Paperbound: 978-1-58549-842-0
Clothbound: 978-0-7884-9344-7

Acknowledgement is made to those who furnished me the desired information to help complete this work. The earlier town records of Cazenovia, covering a most interesting period in its history, have not been preserved; hence much information which might have been gleaned from the early town legislation is irreparably lost. It has been my purpose to collect all available records and present them as accurately as possible in an interesting way so that they may serve as a ready history reference.

Authorities Consulted

"History of Madison County, N. Y." .... Hammond

"History of Chenango and Madison Counties" .... Smith

"Madison County" .... Smith

"Cazenovia" .... Munroe

"First Fifty Years of Cazenovia Seminary" .... Smyth

"My Alma Mater" .... Eddy

Cazenovia Village Newspapers

Village Records

Church Records

CONTENTS

Chapter		Page
I	Founding & Settlement	1
II	Roadways	11
III	Waterways	21
IV	Industries & Institutions	27
V	Religion	41
VI	Education	49
VII	Culture	61

FOUNDING & SETTLEMENT

CAZENOVIA
Past and Present

Chapter I.

Founding and Settlement

Cazenovia, New York, the center town on the western border of Madison County, was founded in 1793.

Until after the close of the Revolutionary War, the territory embraced in the present Chenango and Madison Counties was included in the indefinite Indian domain. In 1788, Governor Clinton effected a treaty with the Indians whereby their title to the major portions of the two counties was extinguished. The next year the Legislature passed an act directing the Surveyor-General to lay out and survey twenty townships. After the completion of the survey, the Commissioners of the Land Office were to select five of the choicest of these twenty townships, which were to be sold only for gold or silver or to redeem certain bonds which the State had issued in the form of bills of credit. They were further required to affix to the lands such price as was best calculated to effect a ready sale, and at the same time ensure the greatest revenue to the State Treasury. The commissioners were required to give three months' public notice of the contemplated sale by advertising in the papers published in the cities of Albany and New York, in the latter of which the sales were to take place. The sales took place, but owing to the brief notice and the imperfect means of travel and communication, they were lightly attended, and the towns in many cases fell naturally, easily and unavoidably into the hands of jobbers and wealthy capitalists, who were in attendance upon legislative action, and always on the alert for lucrative investments, and who immediately advanced the price from three to twenty shillings per acre.

Due to a misapprehension in the survey, there was left between the west line of the Twenty Townships and the east line of the Military Tract a strip which was named the Gore. Two tracts, one of 15,000 acres and one of 41,000 acres were sold off. These two tracts were known as the Road Township, from the fact that the proceeds arising from its sale were to be applied to the construction of roads. This, together with the previous tract, soon after came into possession of the Holland Land Company.

John Lincklaen, Esq., of Amsterdam, Holland, under the patronage of Peter Stadniski, President of the Holland Land Company, was sent into the United States to explore the new countries, and to make a purchase of a tract of land if he should find a suitable situation. Accordingly in the year 1790, he came to America with letters of instruction to the Company's Agent, Theophilus Cazenove, then residing in the city of Philadelphia.

Inspired with zeal for his mission Mr. Lincklaen in the month of September, 1792, having completed his preparation for a tour in the wilderness, employed two hardy woodsmen to accompany him and set out. He ascended the North River to Albany, thence by the Mohawk river to old Fort Schuyler. He then steered off in a westerly direction in the back parts of Herkimer County. His object was to explore the tract of about one hundred thousand acres, being the strip lying between the Military Townships and the tract called the Governors' Purchase of 20 Townships, distinguished on the map of the State of New York as the Road Township, the Gore and No. One of the 20 townships.

In this wilderness the enterprising young Hollander continued with his little company eleven days, enduring all the hardships and privations which such hazardous expeditions are subject to, with only raw pork and bread to subsist upon, and many miles from any inhabitants. He kept a journal of his journey, which, having been translated from the French in which it was originally written, relates that on the afternoon of Thursday, October 11, 1792, he arrived at the foot of the beautiful lake in Cazenovia where his party encamped for the night. As the result of a reconnoiter he wrote: "The situation is superb and the lands are beautiful."

Pleased with the tract and situation, after his arduous undertaking, he returned to Philadelphia and reported to Mr. Cazenove in so favorable a manner the result of his expedition, that the tract was immediately bought and Mr. Lincklaen became the agent with an interest in the purchase.*

The earliest authentic version of the founding of the village is contained in an address made by Mr. S. S. Forman, clerk of the Holland Land Company, on the occasion of the forty-eighth anniversary of the settlement of this section of the Empire State, celebrated on the eighth day of May, 1841. At that time he said:

"Messrs. Cazenove and Lincklaen made me proposals to accompany Mr. Lincklaen to commence his settlement on this tract of land. The negotiation was soon confirmed. Mr. Lincklaen requested me to meet him in New York in April then next. When we met, he gave me his plans fully, and requested me to purchase a complete assortment of goods such

---

*The Village of Cazenovia lies only partially in the tract originally purchased by Mr. Lincklaen, the center of Seminary Street being the north line of that purchase. Afterwards, when it became desirable to use land to the north of this for the village plot, some 10,000 acres of the New Petersburgh Tract were purchased. The southern part of the purchase, however, was not as favorable for cultivation as the northern; it was more liable to frost, and the soil different. It lay, too, out of the direction of the tide of emigration that was then just beginning to roll with great strength and velocity toward the western part of the state.

as I deemed suitable for a new settlement in order to give every facility to the emigrants, observing, that the profits on the goods was of no consideration; but the grand object was to promote the settlement of the lands —that I must not be afraid of buying too much of useful articles—that the company had appropriated $20,000 for the purpose. He added, that if I knew of any mechanics or others who would like to go with us to engage them—I accordingly engaged one carpenter (John Wilson) one mason (Michael Day) one teamster (James Smith). When the North River opened, I shipped all the goods and farming utensils on board of an Albany sloop commanded by Capt. William Schenck, a most worthy Revolutionary officer. Also myself and four hired men I took along. From Albany I sent the men on to old Fort Schuyler (now the city of Utica); the goods I transported by land to Schenectady and then shipped them on board of bateaux and accompanied them myself to old Fort Schuyler. I took passage with them in order to learn how the boatmen managed, and try to discover whether any plan could be devised to prevent pilfering, but alas! there were too many temptations to become rogues if they were ever honest. This was a tedious and vexatious journey of several days—no stage had yet ever started on these roads. At old Fort Schuyler the goods were all stored with John Post, Esq., the only merchant and tavern-keeper at that place, and then only two framed houses. From that place we brought the goods to the Road Township (now Cazenovia) as occasion required and we had a place for them.

"At Ft. Schuyler we hired seven additional men as foresters, viz: James Greene, David Fay, Stephen F. Blackstone, Philemon Tuttle, David Freeborn, Gideon Freeborn and Asa C. Towns. I believe wages were $10 per month and board. I also bought a yoke of oxen, a cart and provisions. On the morning of leaving Utica I weighed out some raw pork and bread to all the men to carry in their knapsacks and an axe apiece to ten of them—and started them and the magazine team on their pilgrimage, on the Great Genesee Road, via the Dean Road so called—Shortly after Mr. Lincklaen and myself started on horseback—I believe we all stayed the first night at Wemples' Tavern at the Indian Mills, near the Oneida Castle. Our journey this day was about twenty miles. The country new, roads bad, much of the way was what is called corduroy road. The next morning we started on our way, continuing on the Genesee road until we crossed Chittenango Creek, about twelve miles—here we turned south and continued about one mile up the creek when we came to a beautiful flat settled by German squatters from the Mohawk River and some Indians. Here we left all settlements and took a blind Indian path bearing westwardly up a steep hill. Now commenced the tug of encountering the dense forest— the axe men commenced opening a road so as to let the cart pass along. By the time that we had ascended the summit of the hill the sun was nearly down; of course time to prepare for the night. By the side of our path lay a trunk of a large tree which had blown down—under the lee of this, with a large fire in front a few paces off, we thought we could be made comfortable. Our cattle and horses being secured and taken care of, we all then repaired to our magazine cart; out with our jack-knives and commenced supper on raw pork and bread—each one helped himself in his own way, some cut long sticks and sharpened one end and put the pork on it and toasted the pork in the fire—After this operation was finished each one wrapped himself in his blanket and stretched himself on the ground by the side of the tree with his feet toward the fire.

"The next morning, 8th of May, 1793, at daylight we arose, brushed the cobwebs from our faces, ate our breakfast on the same sumptuous fare as our supper. It was thought advisable to have another pair of oxen; accordingly one man with my horse was dispatched to Whitestown (upward of 30 miles) to buy and bring on as soon as possible another pair. Mr. Lincklaen now proposed to me that he and I would take his horse and ride and tie* (as the new country phrase is) and go on to the outlet of the lake, by following the Indian path, distant about seven miles, supposing by night that all the company would fetch up with us. When we arrived at the destined spot, we had the pleasure to meet with three men who came there for the purpose of fishing. Their names were Charles Rowe, Joseph Atwell* and Phineas Barnes, all then living in Pompey Hollow, a few miles to the west of this place. The outlet of the lake was so small that a man could step across it. The Indians had constructed a wear to catch fish as they run out of the lake; they had also erected a bark hut near by. On our arrival at this place, we took off the saddle and bridle and portmanteau from the horse and turned him out to feed on the oak plains. It is the practice with the Indians to fire the woods in the Spring of the year, which hastens vegetation and brings early and tender herbage and induces wild beasts to come upon their hunting grounds—here the horse found good pasture. In the evening we five collected in the bark hut. Our people and team did not make their appearance, we two travelers consequently were not provided for with provisions, the three Pompenians discovering our destitute situation, kindly shared their excellent bread and raw pork with us. By this time a friendly introduction took place and they were made acquainted with the object of our business, so a mutual exchange of expression of kind feelings passed. We then set about to arrange affairs

---

*"Riding and tying;" i.e. one ride ahead, and get off, and tie the horse to a bush and walk onward; the one left behind walks until he comes up to the horse, then mounts and rides ahead; and so on alternately.

*The writer is a descendant of this Joseph Atwell, who had brought his family the year before from Connecticut where they had lived some time. One of Joseph's grandsons, George H. Atwell, moved his family from Pompey Hollow to Cazenovia, purchasing a home on Sullivan Street, where he lived nearly forty years.

for the night lodging in the little hut. Our saddle and portmanteau served for our pillows. By the dawn of the morning our three friends disappeared. About seven o'clock Mr. Lincklaen observed to me, that he had best go back; perhaps some misfortune had befallen our people—that he would leave the horse and dog (old Lion) with me. About ten o'clock my stomach admonished me I had best make back tracks too—for the $500 in specie in the portmanteau would not buy me a breakfast, nor was there a human being within several miles of me to my knowledge and alone in the wilderness rendered my situation rather unpleasant. I saddled my horse and had not lead him far before I gladly met Messrs. Jedidiah Jackson and Joseph Yaw, although they were entire strangers to me. They were sent out from the State of Vermont as an exploring committee of a company to try to find a tract of land to settle. These gentlemen had met Mr. Lincklaen on his returning to the people, and he directed them to me. They enquired the way to Township No. 1 (now the Town of Nelson) I directed them the way and proceeded slowly and solitary on my way. The cause of our people's delay was the axle-tree of the cart broke which was a great damage to us. When the whole company arrived on the Patent, Mr. Lincklaen had his marquee pitched for his own family and a very large tent for his hired men—the spot was near the oaks at the south end of the lake.

"The first work was to build a large log dwelling house and store under one roof, and another large house for the work people; both were set in the white oak grove, a little distance apart. Soon after, a warehouse was built in front of the store. The lands were to have been surveyed and laid out in 150 acre farm lots before this time but was not begun. Mr. Lincklaen dispatched James Greene through the wilderness to Oxford, 50 miles off with only a pocket compass for his guide and bread and pork in his knapsack, to bring Mr. Lock, the surveyor, to do his work. By this time some land hunters had come, they were very fortunately employed by Mr. Lock as axemen, chain bearers, etc. This gave them a fine opportunity of sizing the land and selecting lots. The land sales commenced at $1.50 per acre, $10.00 to be paid down—balance in 10 years with interest yearly —the purchaser to clear and sow or plant 10 acres and build a comfortable log cabin on his lot the first year. Mr. Lincklaen gave out word that the first ten families should have one hundred acres each for $1.00 per acre. Two miles were reserved off the north end of the Road Township and laid out in ten acre lots for the benefit of the villagers. The village plot was not laid out until the next summer, 1794. The first job of clearing land, Mr. Lincklaen let 10 acres to James Greene and David Fay, over on the farm now owned by Mr. Tillotson on the west side of the lake.*

*This farm was purchased in 1810 by Ephriam Tillotson and in later years known as the Burr Wendell farm. The writer's grandmother, Orange Tillotson Atwell, was born on and married from this farm.

"Emigration from the neighboring towns was not contemplated, but supposed they would come from 'Down East' but terms were too favorable for the keen Yankee eye to let slip, and before the lots were surveyed and even before the workmen had time to finish their log house for themselves, several respectable families from the towns through which we passed coming from Utica came on as settlers without having previously provided any shelter for their families—our men kindly gave up their tent to their families and sheltered themselves as well as they could in their unfinished house.

"We were informed that some of these families were young married people, who had abbreviated their courtship in order to avail themselves of this favorable opportunity to commence the world. This was Yankee prudence and foresight, without any trick about it. For several weeks our baking and washing was done at old Mrs. Schuyler's at Chittenango Flats. One day Mr. Lincklaen returning from there, brought home with him in his surtout pocket, a kitten, which was the first and only one for a long time. There were no other domestic animals in the settlement except horses, oxen, and two or three dogs.

"The horses and oxen had bells put on them and were turned on the oak plains; toward evening they would all run in from the woods to shelter themselves in the smoke of the settlement to get away from the large horse flies, they were so plentiful that it seemed sometimes they would devour the creatures. This circumstance is well impressed upon the memory, because their stamping and shaking their bells all night under our windows kept sleep away from us. The Holland Company sent to Mr. Lincklaen eight head of Dutch cattle, six of which were cows the size of our oxen; their colors were clear black and white—not spotted but large patches of the two colors—very handsome bodies and straight limbs, horns middling size, but gracefully set. Their necks were seemingly too slender to carry their heads—their disposition mild and docile. For some reason or other, they did not do well and entirely run out. Some supposed that the country was too new, the pasturage different from what they had been accustomed to. The company went to an enormous expense with these cattle, a groom was sent along for the express purpose of taking care of them.

"For several days flights of pigeons (not quail) came over our camp a little before sunset, their flights were so low that we shot them with guns and pistols, and knocked them down with poles and clubs—they were fine ingredients with our pork and made a dish fit for epicures.

"When the surveyor commenced his work, the emigrants followed him so closely that as soon as two sides of a lot could be ascertained and the number known, they would run to the office to have it entered and perhaps a person would have to name several before he could get one. We were obliged to suspend the sales at one time for fear of making mistakes by reason of the competition. The land sales closed the first season I think at $2.00 per acre, on the Road Township, now Cazenovia.

"It was some time after our first arrival before we could be prepared to receive the merchandise which was stored at Utica, and owing to the badness of the roads there was great risk in carting liquors—one time in particular Mr. Lincklaen was in Utica and engaged a respectable trusty farmer to bring out a Hogshead of spirits, the transportation of which cost $10.00. At that time this article was considered as almost indispensable in a new country—we had no faucets, but I tapped the hogshead and put a quill in it, and drew the contents out through the quill as occasion required.

"The first winter I had business in Whitestown and Utica and went in a lumber sleigh, our Jersey teamster and J. Smith drove. On our return we traveled all night being in a hurry to get back. When we arrived at the head of the lake, at the first dawn of the morning, we stopped to examine the ice—it was perfectly transparent—we took our axe (a necessary tool to take along in those days) we cut through the ice and concluded that we should be safe. After we drove on the lake the ice cracked and radiated from the horses' feet in every direction, the horses became frightened—we almost repented our temerity, the driver kept the horses on a good steady trot, we arrived safe at the settlement where we found all the people on the bank of the lake watching with much anxiety for our safety, after they could ascertain what we were. Our first appearance astonished the spectators—some supposed us to be a large bear, some one thing and some another. This probably was the first time that a sleigh and pair of horses was ever driven on this lake.

"In 1794 the village of Cazenovia was laid out by Judge Wright of Rome and Calvin Guiteau of Utica. It was Mr. Lincklaen's wish to have the village laid out on the bank of the lake, and to have a street running on the bank. This it was thought would give a better appearance to the village; but the Company did not own far enough north to adopt that plan. The first sales of village lots were at $5.00, upon certain conditions to build and improve the lots; but they shortly rose higher. Mr. Lincklaen wished to call the village Hamilton—he was a great admirer of General Hamilton, who was at that time Secretary of the Treasury, under George Washington, but the settlers in one of the adjoining townships had named their settlement Hamilton, so the name of Cazenovia was established in honor of Theophilus Cazenove, the Holland Land Company's Agent.*

*The name "Cazenove" appears on a silver name plate on a pew in Christ Church, Alexandria, Virginia, where George Washington worshipped.

"In 1795 I believe it was, Mr. Lincklaen built his first house, about 50 feet square and handsome. The roof of this house was at one time all covered with sheet lead, but it had not the desired effect of keeping it from leaking so it was taken off. The house took fire twice; the second time it was destroyed together with many books and papers containing the early records of the company and a great deal of elegant furniture.* (The site of Mr. Lincklaen's dwelling on the bank of the lake was a picturesque spot and its selection evinced the good taste of its owner. When the house burned in 1806, he chose another site at the foot of the lake, where he erected in 1807 a substantial brick house, commanding a beautiful view of the entire length of the lake. It is still standing, occupied by Mrs. Charles S. Fairchild, who calls the place 'Lorenzo.' Mrs. Fairchild is a descendant of the adopted son of Col. John Lincklaen. Mr. Fairchild, who was Secretary of the United States Treasury under the Cleveland administration, died in 1924. Mr. and Mrs. Fairchild entertained President and Mrs. Cleveland at Lorenzo, where the flower gardens have long been noted for their beauty.)

"A person who never commenced to settle in the wilderness can have but a faint idea of the difficulties, privations and hardships attending such a life. No doubt but the children of Israel had hard times. This settlement commenced under the most auspicious circumstances—the land cheap, credit long, a fatherly patronage almost; no one of these settlers was ever reduced to the necessity of going from home for the necessarys of life. This was no ordinary beginning, it has been providentially a felicitous one; happiness has generally reigned throughout. In all our meetings, whether of a public nature or for innocent amusement and recreation, the utmost harmony and decorum ever prevailed. Coming together as we did from all points of the compass, the intelligence of the American character was at all times conspicuous. In our little gatherings a dignity and propriety of conduct was observed that would have been creditable to a more polished society.

"Where can we find a better country in all respects than this which we now inhabit—scarcely a 150 acre lot but what is well watered with delightful streams—the soil good, country healthy, turnpikes and town roads in every direction and kept in good order, rendering travel safe and pleasant. The village is so happily situated from the great thoroughfares of the railroads as to be free from the demoralizing effects of corrupt populations which are to be found in such places. This place is so situated that it has no rival to contend with—in short, this section of country seems to be a little world by itself and each one seems to be contented with his own business.

---

*The John Lincklaen marker, just inside the entrance to the Owahgena Clubhouse grounds, indicates the location of this first house.

" 'All separate, yet harmonizing well and mingled with each other,
One whole in several parts, yet each part spreading to a whole.
A union of action, for the good of the whole, the contracted
Thought of meum and teum, yet lies dormant in the hidden bosom.'

"In the year 1822 the settlement had the misfortune to lose Col. Lincklaen, the Father and Patron of the place."

ROADWAYS

Chapter II.

Roadways

When the first settlers came in there was not a road in the county. There were two principal routes by which they came, the north and south water routes—the former, the Hudson and Mohawk rivers; the latter, the Susquehanna; and the most navigable streams were the most frequented highways for some years after they arrived. Many, however, compassed the entire distance from the far New England states on foot, bringing nothing with them but an axe. Those who came with their families generally came with ox teams drawing sleds, sometimes wood-shod, or covered wagons, often performing the entire journey in this manner and frequently driving a few sheep, cattle and other animals before them. Many, however, resorted to this mode of conveyance only to and from the termini of the water routes. The winter season was generally selected as then they could reach points in the wilderness which were inaccessible to their rude conveyances at other seasons.

Many who came by the northern route threaded forests unbroken from Whitestown, except by the few scant, rude clearings made by the Indians. Blazed trees were the forest guide boards, and by their aid the forests were traversed from one locality to another. But these human denizens could not prosper in their isolated settlements; they must needs open communication with each other, and to this end roads were indispensable and of the first importance. The pioneers first followed the Indian trails and from these branched off into routes indicated by marked trees. The earliest authentic representation of these trails indicates one extending southwest from the Mohawk at about the locality of Utica, through Oneida to Cazenovia Lake and thence westward.

It need not excite our wonder that in those days people were anxious for better and speedier means of communication, a better means of getting from and to the new settlements. As a turnpike road at that day was regarded as furnishing the best possible facilities for postal and commercial intercourse, turnpike companies were early formed to afford the desired relief. The turnpike fever was as virulent in its day as was the plank road fever at a later day.

Our first settlers came in by the Genesee Turnpike north of us, so our first roads ran north to connect with it. To unite the inhabitants of the more northern portions of the county, to make easy their communication with eastern friends, and to facilitate their market journeyings, the Peterboro turnpike, extending from Cazenovia, through Peterboro to Vernon, was laid out in 1804. A road was soon built to the older settlement of Pompey Hill.

Local roads were rapidly opened in the various towns. The Holland Land Company opened the following roads at the commencement of the settlement, viz:

1. From Chittenango to Cazenovia.
2. From Cazenovia to Manlius Square.
3. From Cazenovia south to the branch office in Brakel.
4. From Cazenovia through the first and second towns, eastwardly to go to Utica via Paris, and New Hartford.
5. From Cazenovia to Pompey Hollow.
6. From Cazenovia, on the east side of the lake, to intersect the Genesee Road near the "Deep Springs."

The necessities of other towns, however, required for them a more direct communication with the outer world, so the "Third Great Western Turnpike" or the more familiar name of "Cherrry Valley Turnpike" was the result of these needs. Col. Lincklaen, who was the president of the turnpike, was the principal person in causing it to be built from Cherry Valley to Manlius Square. The turnpike has proved to be a most important benefit to the country through which it passes, but was unfortunate for the original stockholders.

A coach road, begun in 1799, from Albany to Cherry Valley, had been completed. The enterprising prime movers in the grand scheme of constructing a good wagon road from Cherry Valley to Manlius, through towns and counties of dense forests, over the most hilly country known outside of veritable mountainous districts, with no rich towns along the route to bond, or even to aid them by subscription, formed a company, went courageously into the work, obtained a charter in 1803 and completed the grand enterprise in 1811 at a cost of over $90,000. Cazenovia men were foremost in the great work, devoting their time and investing their capital without prospect of full compensation. The turnpike brought Cazenovia into special notice and placed it on an equal footing with towns of established reputation further east; no village in the county had greater consequence and influence than this. All roads, such as they were, then led to Cazenovia—Cazenovia was on the great highway to the west; it was in the public eye. It has become a strong trading center; it had more business, more manufacturing industries and a greater population than any other village in the county. The selection of Cazenovia as the county seat in 1810 and its continuance as such during seven years doubtless also contributed in some degree to the business importance of the village.

When the Cherry Valley Turnpike was completed to Manlius where it connected with the Genesee turnpike, the embargo was raised and everything desirable in facilities for travel seemed to be accomplished. It was not at that time supposed that better facilities for travel could ever be provided. A line of stages was run, "Four Horse Post Coaches" they were called by the Postoffice Department, and no one was allowed to carry the mails without means for conveying passengers. When a turnpike had a line of stage coaches run upon it it seemed that improvement in that direction had found its utmost limit. But some thought the world was being turned upside down and that all the wealth of the country would be in the grasp of aristocratic stage proprietors and the bloated turnpike stockholders, insomuch that the liberties our fathers "fout" for would be seriously endangered. Some considered the turnpike a nuisance, as letting an undesirable class of people into the country, besides opening it to the importation of all the foreign knicknacks and they had no doubt there had been as much as a cartload of crockery brought into town. The outlook was appalling.

A stage passenger was considered to be above the common herd and was charged double price for what he had at the tavern. Those who used to sit in front of Hikok's tavern (now Cazenovia House) during intermissions of the meeting Sunday noon saw Jerry White, who drew the reins over the foaming steed for many a long year, drive up with prolonged toot of horn and crack of whip. The landlord would open the door of the coach, let down the steps and assist the exhausted people, who were sufficiently wealthy to afford a ride in a stage coach, into the sitting room, the wonder of the gazing crowd of children of all ages from ten to fourscore years. Then might be seen the obsequious landlord with a salver containing goblets of prepared beverages to renew the flagging spirits of the aristocratic, but wearied stage passengers.

Meanwhile the "lackeys" that always hung around the tavern, would bring water for Jerry to water his team of which he would allow each one a prudent share, rubbing their noses with it first, adjusting their headstalls, and portions of the harness that seemed misplaced. Then a boy would bring the Great Western Mail from the postoffice nearby which he would toss up to Jerry to be deposited under his seat. When "all 'board" would ring out in stentorian tones, the refreshed passengers would resume their seats in the coach, Jerry placing the four reins properly between his fingers, the long lash of the whip would crack like a horse pistol, and away with dashing speed would go this most brilliant equipage, the stage coach. How boys used to crave and aspire to be elevated to the position of stage driver! Two days and nights were required to reach Albany, one hundred and thirteen miles distant.

Toll-gates were established every ten miles, so when the traveler had made the trip from the western to the eastern terminus and responded to the many money demands of the toll-gate keepers on the way he had paid a good round sum for his passport. Yet the old highway was traversed daily by a motley throng of people and every conceivable type of vehicle common to those days.

Population increased with wonderful rapidity and the public means of transportation were inadequate to meet the demands upon them. They were supplemented by private freight wagons, which carried to Albany the surplus productions of the farms and returned laden with merchandise. A caravan of teams from a neighborhood would go in company and assist each other, by doubling teams up steep hills and through the deep sloughs. These long journeys, the round trip often occupying two weeks, were thus cheered by mutual aid and sympathy, and were rather interesting episodes in the routine of early farm life. At the hospitable inns, which arose by the wayside every few miles, these hardy and happy teamsters would pass a noon, or night, as cheerfully as any modern traveler in the pretentious hotels of today. Besides these farm teams, heavy transportation wagons were run, often drawn by seven, sometimes nine horses, and carrying a proportionate load. The wagons were massive, with very broad-tired wheels, to prevent them from penetrating the road bed. It was no uncommon thing to see long strings of these farm wagons, laden with produce, approaching some central and important mart, to the number of fifty or a hundred. In 1804 the settlers sent cattle to Philadelphia in payment for land. A pair of oxen brought $64 and it cost $5 to send them. Farmers along the road profited from the pasturage of droves of catttle. It was worth $2 per hundred to transport goods to Albany.

One of the veteran stage coach drivers was George Shute of Cazenovia, who drove for over sixty years, his route being to Manlius and return. The Syracuse stage met him at Manlius to transfer the mail. His stage coach is in existence and will doubtless become a part of Henry Ford's collection. A timetable for the Cazenovia-Syracuse route, dated April 10, 1860, reads:

"Cazenovia, Manlius and Syracuse

A DAILY STAGE (Sundays excepted) will LEAVE CAZENOVIA at 6:30 A. M. for Syracuse, passing through the following places: Oran, Manlius, Fayetteville and Orville.

Leaving Manlius at 8 A. M. and Fayetteville at 8:30 A. M., arriving at Syracuse at 10 A. M. in time for the Express Train going East, without fail. Returning, will leave Syracuse at 3 P. M., arriving at Manlius at 5 P. M. and at Cazenovia at 6:30 P. M.

The STAGE will connect at Manlius with stage for Delphi on Tuesdays, Thursdays and Saturdays.

Office—Brintnall's Hotel, Syracuse; Fox's Hotel, Manlius; Jewell's Hotel, Cazenovia."

A new coach was put on the Syracuse-Cazenovia route in 1864, which excelled in beauty, convenience and comfort anything in the stage coach line. The body was hung on thorough braces, and finished with great elegance. It cost $1,000. The road to Chittenango was built to give us an outlet to the canals. In 1866 a stage line was run from Cazenovia to Chittenango Station and another one to DeRuyter.

Present day motor traffic demands the best possible roads. The United States Government is mapping out transcontinental routes. The Cherry Valley Turnpike, formerly a part of route 7 in this state, becomes a section of route 20 of the transcontinental highways. Route 20 starts at Boston, passing through Massachusetts to Albany, thence along the Cherry Valley Turnpike to Cazenovia. There on to Auburn, passing south of Buffalo and directly across country to Chicago. From there the route crosses Nebraska and passes on to Yellowstone National Park. In passing over the Rocky Mountains it becomes a part of route 30, eventually following the course of the Columbia River to the Pacific Ocean. Route 20 is the only transcontinental route passing through New York State. It was doubtless the intention at the start to run the Cherry Valley Turnpike over the hill at the foot of Cazenovia Lake, into Pompey Hollow, over the continuous hills and into the intervening valleys, that might well discourage even a more energetic class of men and it would have rendered the road at that time and for the immediate purpose wanted, nearly worthless. The work of completing the unimproved stretch from Cazenovia to Auburn was begun in the Spring of 1927.

The Cherry Valley Turnpike Association was formed in September, 1926. Its purpose is to exploit the historic turnpike, to protect and advance the interests of it as the most attractive motor route between Albany and Syracuse as to distance, running time, freedom from congested traffic and scenic beauty.

Concrete roads radiate north, east and south of Cazenovia. During 1926-27, a concrete road was built on the Chittenango Falls road from the High Bridge to the village, the course of the road being changed from the west side of the creek to the east side, from the bridge to the top of the Falls, through the State Park. This road affords a much more beautiful view of the Falls than the old road did. "Hiawatha Trail" has been suggested as an appropriate name for the new state road. Hiawatha was the father of the first League of Nations, the Iroquois Confederation of Indian tribes.

The following interesting article written by Mrs. Roy D. Armstrong of West Winfield, N. Y., is reproduced here by permission:

"Hush! Listen! Look out of the window and listen! Perhaps the old Cherry Valley Turnpike has a message for you. I'll try to tell its story as it has seemed to tell it to me.

"I'm an old, old trail awinding from Albany to Syracuse, called the Cherry Valley Turnpike. I like that old word 'Turnpike.' It means a road on which are toll-gates, but tho' the last toll-gate has long since been torn from my side, the old name still lingers, for which I am glad. I am also known as Route No. 20. When I was young I was called the Great Western Turnpike, but as more roads were built to the west and perhaps also to distinguish me from my neighbor, the Skaneateles Turnpike, I was called the 'Cherry Valley' and that is the name I prefer. What memories that name brings to my mind, the saddest in all my long history.

>'Hark! Hark! Methinks I hear some melancholy moan,
>Stealing upon my listening ear,
>As though some departing spirit were about
>To soar, amid the horrors of a massacre!
>Yes, the savage fiend, with glittering knife
>And tomahawk, reeking with infant blood,
>Stands in awful prospect before my vision.'

"November eleventh is now celebrated as Armistice Day, but to me it has another meaning, for it was the morning of November 11, 1778 that I saw the Indians and Tories steal down from the wooded hills, where they had hidden during the night, and begin their terrible slaughter. I was only a road and helpless to aid what had been my most prosperous settlement. How well I remember it! The enemy had learned from a scout which they had taken, that the officers of the garrison lodged in private houses outside the fort, as the settlement had thought itself secure.

"Col. Alden and Lieut. Col. Stacia, with a small guard, lodged at Mr. Wells'. A Mr. Hamble was coming on horseback from his house several miles below and when a short distance from Mr. Wells' house was fired upon and wounded by the Indians. He rode in great haste to inform Col. Alden of their approach and then hastened to the fort. The Rangers stopped to examine their fire-locks, the powder in which had been wet by the rain. The Indians, improving this opportunity, rushed by. The advance body was composed principally of Senecas, at that time the wildest and most ferocious of the Six Nations.

"Col. Alden made his escape from the house and was pursued toward the fort by an Indian who threw his tomahawk and struck him on the head and then rushed up and scalped him. Lieut. Col. Stacia was taken prisoner. The guards were all killed or captured. The Wells family were all killed, leaving one son who was away at school. A Tory boasted that he killed Mr. Wells while at prayer.

"Mrs. Dunlop, the minister's wife, was killed in the doorway of her home, but Rev. Samuel Dunlop and a daughter were saved by a friendly Mohawk, though Mr. Dunlop died about a year later as the result of the shock of that day. Thirty-two inhabitants, mostly women and children, were killed, and sixteen Continental Soldiers. Many were taken prisoner and others escaped to come creeping back a few days later to a desolate scene, as every building in Cherry Valley had been burned.

"But my memories are not all sad ones. In 1798, I was considered very popular as there were twenty four-in-hands each way going over me every day and inns were placed at my side a mile apart. In my early days, what is now Guilderland, eight miles from Albany, was known as 'The Glass House' in memory of the fact that Alexander Hamilton once established there the manufacture of glass. Here was 'Sloan's' a famous tavern. In its low barns was stabling for three hundred horses and the inn could accommodate a like number of guests, but of not one bath room did it boast. Those were the days of the 'Covered Wagon.' How many families have I seen pass over me on their way to form a new home in the Genesee Valley, or to journey farther west. They took with them all of their worldly goods and how strange would look their oxen drawn vehicles if they were to appear on me today.

"As I see cattle riding over me in comfortable trucks, I recall the droves of other days and the tired cattle and their drovers who had walked many weary miles for many days perhaps. Each night a farmer must be found who would rent a pasture, but that was not difficult as that was a regular business with the farmers who lived beside me.

"Droves of sheep there were also, sometimes a thousand, a slow-moving, compact, bleating mass. And the flocks of turkeys! Imagine if you can several hundred turkeys being driven two hundred miles or more to Albany. The driver rode in front on a horse and from a bag of corn, scattered a trail of kernels, which the turkeys followed unerringly all day, but as soon as it began to grow dark all would fly to the nearest trees and no amount of persuasion could induce them to go a rod farther until morning.

"Many were the loads of produce that went to Albany. Butter in wooden firkins, bundles of wool, a little flax and cakes of tallow, while the returning load brought molasses, codfish, some calico and sometimes a piece of silk for the wedding gown of the daughter of the household.

"Many were the horseback riders and often a lady fair rode behind on the horse. But the stage coaches and their four shining horses were the admiration and excitement of the day. How fast they traveled—eight miles per hour. How little I thought then that I would see the time when automobiles would rush over me at sixty miles per hour, but no Pierce Arrow nor Marmon of today causes the thrill that did the passing of the stage coach in those bygone days.

"Many old roads have outlived their usefulness, but not so with me as I never was so popular as at the present time. A score of years ago I feared that I had seen my best days; in some places grass was growing in my midst, but with the coming of the auto all this has changed. Now that an Association has been formed to do me honor, I can but feel proud and happy and look with hope toward even better days to come.

"Time has indeed wrought great changes. I have seen the ox-cart give place to the horse and carriage and later replaced by the automobile. Inns came and went and now have sprung up again twenty fold. The hitching-post has been taken down to make room for the gasoline tank. The blacksmith shop has become a garage. And when I think of the 'Hot Dog' stands I sometimes wonder what a road may come to.

"The covered wagon belongs to the past, but the spirit that in it moved westward with the sun, still finds expression among people, to whom new lands are no longer possible, in trying to make better the land in which they dwell."

THE OLD TOLL GATE

It stood about two miles west of Morrisville, on the old Cherry Valley turnpike, which was at that time the only correct route to Cazenovia. Recollections of it date back to the early forties before the California gold fever had struck the United States or the railroads or telegraphs had struck the world; and the dirt roads were the only avenues for climbing about the country. Just how the old toll house looked and the old toll gate and all of the surroundings is engraved in memory as distinctly as a photograph and as indelible as a blot of axle grease on a pair of white duck pantaloons.

"There is a memory comes from the dim, distant past,
   When the world and its people didn't travel as fast
   As they do in these days of lightning and steam;
   When everything goes on a gallop, it would seem.
   Then railroads and telegraphs were unknown in the land,
   And people who traveled had to travel by hand.
   They jogged and they jolted over rough rocky roads,
   On horseback and in wagons made for carrying loads.
   Then light running buggies and fast trotting teams,
   Were things never dreamed of in our most fanciful dreams.
   The lumbering stage coach with its thorough-brace springs,
   Was considered the acme of elegant things.
   And the long lines of travel to the east and the west;
   Went over the dirt roads that were shortest and best.
   The old fashioned turnpike was a thoroughfare then,
   For long droves of cattle and of migrating men.
   And along down the line were stations and gates,
   Where travelers paid toll at the advertised rates.
   How the old toll house looked to my mind now appears,

And the old man who had tended for a long line of years.
With his broad brimmed felt hat and his old fashioned clothes,
And his massive steel spectacles astride of his nose.
The old man was peculiar, but an honest old soul,
As he stood by his gate post and pulled in the toll.
And each one that came by most certainly knew,
That he must come down with the dust or he couldn't go through.
But the lordly old stage driver made his every day trip,
He was proud of his team, but more proud of his whip.
The gate would fly open when the stage would appear,
He wouldn't stop for the toll for he paid by the year.
And the long droves of cattle, of sheep and of swine,
Couldn't go with a rush, but must march through in a line.
He would not leave the score number to a guess or surmise;
But he counted them all with his spectacled eyes.
When he took in a shilling, or a dollar or a dime,
It went into the cash box for the road every time.
The old man had been there so many long years;
That his habits were fixed as firm as his ears.
When the sunset occurred as it did every day,
One could see him come out in his habitual way,
With his watch in his hand and his almanac by his side,
To observe if his watch or his almanac lied.
And he knew without fail when he looked at the sky,
If the next day would be wet or would it be dry.
He would stand there in the twilight at the close of the day,
And gossip with any travelers that were passing that way.
And if he felt like it he would kindly unfold
All the news in his paper a week or two old.
The old man went to Heaven many long years ago,
And the toll gate went where such thing always go.
And those who travel that road with their hurrying ways,
Have no thought of those tolls of those long ago days."

WATERWAYS

CHAPTER III.

Waterways

The location of the village must be regarded as a fortunate one, being 1,250 feet above sea level and almost surrounded by water; the lake on the west, the outlet of the lake on the south, while to the east and north flows Chittenango Creek.*

Cazenovia Lake is the principal inland body of water in Madison County, and is one of the most beautiful minor sheets of water in the state. Viewing the country about the village from the high ground at the head of Sullivan Street, one sees on every side, except the south, that the hills have a gentle descent, forming somewhat the make of a valley, and yet the lake is four and a half miles long, from a half mile to a mile wide and about sixty feet deep. It discharges its waters into Chittenango Creek which was a feeder for the Erie canal. It occupies an elevated basin 900 feet above tidewater and is fed apparently by springs as there is no inlet to supply the water wider than one can step over and the outlet is large except in very dry seasons. When a traveler arrives, he is greeted, as it were, with the smiles of a beautiful sheet of water, seemingly basking in the sun on the summit of the land—the fish in their element and the inhabitants of the village basking in the sunshine of prosperity on the earth.

The lake is well stocked with fish; perch, trout, sunfish and bullheads are native. At one time 43 small pickerel measuring about four to nine inches long were brought from Leland's Pond in Eaton, and put in the lake. An agreement was made by the inhabitants that no person would take any within three years. At the expiration of that time they had multiplied beyond all expectations and were in abundance, but they destroyed the smaller fry, except the horny bullheads. The lake, formerly called Lincklaen Lake, also bears the Indian name "Owahgena" meaning "The lake of the yellow perch."

Cazenovia, like many other towns in the county, is rich in incidents suggestive of the occupancy of this region of country by a race of people anterior to those from whom the present inhabitants are descended. In various localities, and notably so at the head and upon the outlet of the lake, the plow has disclosed evidences that the aborigines camped with more or less permanency and at places in considerable numbers, and pursued their domestic avocations, hunted, fished, trapped, tilled and buried their dead; while to the west of the foot of the lake is a locality of no little inter-

---

*"Chittenango" means "waters divide and run north." It is a corruption of the Oneida Indian name meaning, "Where the sun shineth out."

est to antiquarians, known as Indian Fort.* It is situated on the west line of the town, partly in Cazenovia and partly in Pompey, upon a slight eminence, nearly surrounded by a deep ravine.

Previous to the treaties of 1788, the lake was the especial property of the Oneida Indians, who had established themselves near the head of it. They were undoubtedly one of the six families of the great Confederacy which may have been driven from here at last by some invading foe or perhaps they abandoned their fortifications for some more congenial spot. At any rate, in September, 1861, a sunken canoe or "dug out," filled with stones, was discovered in the lake by a party of three gentlemen fishing. They succeeded in getting the canoe to the surface and towing it ashore. Its antique appearance excited much interest among the Cazenovians, and thereupon was kindled a flame of enthusiasm for the departed nobility of the race once the unquestioned lords of Lake Owahgena, who had sunk their canoes that the invading foe might not possess them. It was decided to return the relic to its bed of aquatic weeds, where it had evidently long rested, with ceremonials befitting the occasion. Accordingly, on the 12th day of the succeeding October, all Cazenovia gathered at the lake to witness the unique proceedings, in which thirty-one persons from among the most prominent citizens, dressed in aboriginal costume, took part. The Indians who were dwellers of these localities had mostly disappeared before the advent of the white settlers in 1792.

There was a thrill of pride and pleasure among the early inhabitants of the village when the first little steamboat was built and launched in 1808. Other and larger boats came later, and so for many years the lake was not without steam craft. There was a $2,500 steamer on the lake in 1870. Two years later, a small steamboat named "Lottie," which was about thirty feet long and would carry thirty or forty passengers, was launched. Lake fetes, or regattas, were held often. As many as forty sail and oar boats filled with "beaux and beauties" glided over its surface to music on the water. The steamer was trimmed in colors; the boats, decorated with Chinese and colored lanterns and flags, moving about, reminded one of the Venetian gondolas with their beautiful reflections in the water. Fire works were sent up from the middle of the lake.

The beauties of Owahgena Lake are portrayed in the following verses by Rev. Dwight Williams:

---

*Also known as Atwell fort. Joseph Atwell was first white settler on adjoining land.

Owahgena, I have seen
All thy moods from storm to sheen
Parked about with avenues
Leading to thy charming views,
Nook, and cove, and lawns of green,
Villas, which a reigning queen
Far from courts or royal mien
Might for rest and beauty choose,
  Owahgena.
Here old forests' monarchs lean
O'er thy crystal depths serene,
Where thy spray-like crystal dews
Bathes their feet, or sparkling, woos
Summer birds that come to preen,
  Owahgena.

 Nearly the entire shore line of the lake is owned now by private interests. Summer homes, with expansive green lawns, have been built; a few camps on either side, a club-house at the outlet, a public pier where the village has a pumping station to force the spring water from the lake to the reservoir some distance away. The village also owns a small park space on the east shore where picnics are held, auto campers may rest, and bathers have the freedom of the water. Before the extensive use of manufactured ice, the lake supplied a large part of Syracuse as well as Cazenovia with ice.

 Chittenango Creek rises in the highlands of Fenner and Nelson, eventually emptying into Oneida Lake. It presents in its course some rare scenes of romantic beauty, and is altogether the most important stream in the county for hydraulic purposes. Between Cazenovia and Chittenango it possesses as convenient and uniform a water power as exists in the State. Every portion of this eight miles may be conveniently used for hydraulic purposes. The descent is somewhat more than 740 feet, with one perpendicular fall of 134 feet at Chittenango Falls, where the water plunges in a beautiful cascade, over a ledge of limestone rock.

 Under Governor Smith, the property around the Falls, which had been held for some time by private interests, presumably to prevent the water power from being commercialized, became a state park. It is intended to include in this park land between the Falls and Sulphur Springs.

 A stranger, coming to Cazenovia on the stage coach in 1865 said, "The road from Chittenango to Cazenovia is charmingly picturesque and wild. It conducts one to a village of white cottages and green blinds, among avenues of maple and elm and perfect bowers of shrubbery."

S. S. Forman, in a letter to the village trustees in 1851 said, "The outlet of the lake, uniting in the mill-pond with Chittenango Creek furnishing a never-failing head of water, forms fine sites for hydraulic purposes, the whole distance capable of propelling machinery at every few rods, which it seems your enterprising citizens have already to a considerable extent improved for years past, and all the distance made of easy access by a plank road through a valley which was formerly considered wholly waste land. The prospect now is that you will become a large manufacturing city that will vie with Lowell. Also your reputed valuable medicinal springs lately brought into public notice and already in high estimation. Those Springs and the hydraulic establishments will mutually aid each other."

A Syracuse physician started a hotel at Sulphur Springs. There were four or five cottages connected with it with full accommodations for families. Many invalids enjoyed the comforts of the place, as well as the medicinal properties of the water.

INDUSTRIES & INSTITUTIONS

CHAPTER IV.

Industries and Institutions

Various manufacturing industries which depended largely on the splendid water power of Chittenango Creek were early established. Cazenovia was noted for manufactures at a day when other towns were only making slow progress in agriculture.

In the summer of 1794 the first grist mill was built by the Land Company. Wheat was bought in Whitestown and other places, ground, and the flour sold so low as only to cover cost and charges for the benefit of the settlers. This mill and a nearby brewery were burned down some years later. Before the first saw mill was built one mile south of the settlement, the boards to finish the log cabins were brought from Capt. Jackson's saw mill in Manlius. The road from Cazenovia to Manlius was first opened for the purpose of carting the boards.

Other industries were the tanning of hides, making of potash, gathering of ginseng and making of nails. Then followed two cloth-dressing establishments, two carding machines, a brewery and distillery; trip-hammer works, a woolen mill, a hat and chair factory, an oil mill, a fulling mill, a shoe manufactory and a lock manufactory. A paper mill was established in 1801 and there was then a great demand for potash kettles. A sash, door and blind factory, a mower and reaper foundry, a morocco factory, other saw and grist mills were conducted. Still later, the manufacture of glass-ball traps, cabinet ware, butter, cheese, wagons, cider and gunpowder was carried on. The merchants of the thirties, forties and fifties did a large business. There was then a home market for every pound of wool, butter and cheese and every bushel of grain. Factories lined the outlet of the lake and Cazenovia was a live business town. Railway communications with the outside world instead of lumbering stage coach and the advent of steam and electricity as motive powers in place of water took away the factories. Since then, manufacturing in Cazenovia has been discouraged with the idea of keeping the village strictly residential. Agriculture has been encouraged and developed to a high degree. Smooth meadows, well cultivated fields, cleanly kept woodlands, first class farm buildings and the evidences of wealth everywhere, on the hills as well as in the valleys, proclaim skilled training in agriculture. Cazenovia is one of the largest dairy towns in Madison County.

Today finds an electric light plant, a canning factory and a telephone system; a machine shop which makes a milk bottle capping machine and special machinery, and a diepress company, which turns out milk bottle caps, milk tickets, tea-tags and tea package ends. Three blacksmith's shops, handed down from one family to another, are still doing a little business although the advent of the automobiles and tractors leaves few horses to be shod. The first blacksmith shop was built of logs. No tongs could be found amongst the smith's tools so Elnathan Andrews, the first blacksmith employed, had to go to Morehouse's Flats, twelve miles off, to borrow a pair.

The village also boasts a Post Office, a National Bank, five churches, a library, several fraternal organizations, a town hall, three hotels, a union school, and the far-famed Cazenovia Seminary; a weekly newspaper, a fire department, a "Village Green," three cemeteries, a golf course, two railroad connections, improved roads, beautiful trees and an air of culture and social distinction found in few small communities.

The first Post Office in Cazenovia was established by Mr. Habersham, then Postmaster General. The country was so little known that he would not establish an office without security that it should not become a charge upon the general Post-Office. Col. Lincklaen and Mr. Forman gave the required security so Mr. Forman was appointed postmaster and the office was kept in his store. The office now requires, besides the postmaster, an assistant and three clerks.

The first bank was the Madison County Bank, organized under the safety fund act, March 14, 1831. Today it is the Cazenovia National Bank, with a million and a half dollars on deposit.

The village supports an excellent public library containing over eighteen thousand volumes. The library undoubtedly had its beginning in the "Free Reading Room Association," formed in 1873 by a small group of people who secured a room, free of charge, in the Burr block, and drew up regulations to the effect that the use of the reading room should be free to any person, resident or stranger, without any fee, who would conform to the regulations as published. As the association was designed to be free to all, it depended on the contributions of the citizens who felt an interest in whatever served to promote the intelligence and good morals of the community. Contributions of newspapers, periodicals and the loan of pictures were acceptable. There was to be an annual membership fee of one dollar.* Five months later the rooms were closed for the summer, due to lack of funds and attendance. The next month, Mr. Krumbhaar gave his sail-boat to be sold for the benefit of the Reading Room, thereby insuring the reopening of the rooms for the winter. There appears no further record of the existence of the association. During the next summer, the Seminary Reading Room was opened to the public.

In January, 1886, an organization formed and incorporated for the

---

*Among the names of the twenty-eight men who joined the Association is that of G. H. Atwell, the writer's grandfather.

purpose of having a circulating library, free to all, where, by a small payment, people could have the use of the books at home and in the library rooms. It was started without any capital, depending on friends to assist by money or books. One hundred volumes were soon pledged and several persons became life patrons by the payment of $10. The same room that had been offered the Free Reading Room Association was again offered free of charge. Mr. R. J. Hubbard gave a deed to the present library property to the trustees of the Library on Nov. 30, 1892. There is no record stating when the Library was transferred to the present building, but it is presumed it was moved from the Burr block at that time. Subscriptions and benefits have helped maintain the expenses. The village appropriated $100 to the Library in 1898. Since 1899, $200 have been given each year, but being insufficient to meet the requirements of the present needs, the village voted in March, 1927, to raise by tax $1,000 yearly for the support of the library. A portrait of Theophilus de Cazenove, presented to the village by his great-grandson, hangs in the Library.

The Masonic order closely follows in the footsteps of the pioneers in every part of the country. During the fall of 1798, eight Masonic brethren of this section conferred with each other and arranged for the organization of United Brethren Lodge No. 78, which charter was granted January 5, 1799. Robert R. Livingston, one of the signers of the warrant, was one of the committee which drafted the Declaration of Independence, and afterwards administered the oath of office to George Washington as the first President of the United States. The Lodge convened May 9, 1799, it being the first lodge in the county. The nearest lodge west of here was at Canandaigua. The early meetings of the lodge were commenced in the afternoon and continued during the evening, each member present contributing to the evening's entertainment. Supper was twenty-five cents. The charter of U. B. Lodge was surrendered in 1839. The anti-Masonic agitation had begun at this time, bringing days of storm and stress; political parties were divided, life-long friendships sundered by reason of it. Lodges were closed, charters surrendered; the order seemed to be ruined. But an order that had survived through centuries of time, an order which was spread throughout the world, was not to be destroyed by a local combination of politicians and fanatics. A chapter of Royal Arch Masons was organized in Cazenovia in 1825. The questions of Masonry and Slavery were rocks on which nearly every Northern church split. In 1828, three Baptist brethren were tried for being Masons. Two were acquitted after having given satisfactory promises not to further affiliate with the order. The church passed a resolution not to admit any more Masons to membership. In 1866 the works of Masonry were resumed in this place; in that year a dispensation was granted and in 1867 a warrant was granted to Cazenovia Lodge 616.

Owahgena Lodge, I. O. O. F. was organized in 1845. The lodge went down in 1860 when everything belonging to it was destroyed by fire. Owahgena Lodge No. 450 was instituted and chartered in 1876; Lincklaen Lodge No. 900 was instituted in 1906. The Daughters of the American Revolution organized in 1896; the Knights of Columbus in 1906. The Eastern Stars organized in 1908; Rebecca Lodge, I. O. O. F. in 1910 and the American Legion in 1920.

The sum of $4,000 was voted in 1854 for building a hall for village meetings. The village was to have right of perpetual use of the basement for the fire department. The Free Church building was bought, enlarged and refurnished. The plan of the hall called for an ample stage, adjacent retiring rooms, a hall with comfortable seats for 500 persons on the second floor. This was to be used for fairs, concerts, elections, political meetings and public assemblies of all kinds. The first floor was to be occupied by a room for justices' courts, a jury room, supper room, etc. This was called the Concert Hall. The Casa Nova (New Hall) was rebuilt from the Concert Hall in 1885-6 and burned down in 1895. Cazenovia Hall, or Town Hall, was built in 1897 by a stock company at a cost of $12,000. The village corporation leases from the association a commodious office for its business and records. The hall is used for public entertainments.

The record of possible tavern keepers in the first quarter of the century is not complete, but it is known that one Ebenezer Johnson kept a hotel in 1799, which was located on the south side of the "Green," and in 1803, Hiram Roberts, a blacksmith, added to his trade the keeping of a tavern. The Cazenovia House has a history going back to about 1810. It was known for forty years or more as the "Drover's Hotel," it being the stopping place of many cattle drivers passing back and forth along the Cherry Valley Turnpike. Cattle were then taken on foot down the turnpike to Madison and thence on to New York. The hotel was known in every quarter and ranked high among country hotels. Simon C. Hitchcock kept the hotel in 1824 and was regarded a first rate landlord. He was also a Seminary trustee. Samuel White kept a hotel on the south side of the square. He was a very agreeable man and kept a very good house.

The Lincklaen House* was built in 1835 by a stock company. It was operated from 1853 to 1877 by a Mr. Jewell and was the stopping place of the stage-coach. It was purchased in 1916 by Mr. Henry Burden who remodeled and modernized it. Many noted guests have been entertained by the hotel. What was formerly the Lake House, now a furniture store and undertaking establishment, was in operation in 1865. This may be the same hotel as that kept by Samuel White in 1824 and the Madison County Hotel which was on the south side of the square in 1879. The hotel kept by Mr.

*The bricks used in the construction of the Lincklaen House were made in Pompey Hollow by Abraham Tillotson, great-great-grandfather of the writer.

Hitchcock on the north side of the square in 1824 doubtless is the same as the "Hikok's Tavern" spoken of elsewhere, now the Cazenovia House. Shoreacres, on the east side of the lake, was converted from a private residence to a popular hotel in 1923. There are three or four attractive tearooms.

The first newspaper in the village was "The Pilot," started in 1808. Since then there have been numerous publications, some short and some long lived. The Whigs, Tories, Republicans and Democrats have all had their say. The present Cazenovia Republican was established in 1854.

Cazenovia has always had an efficient fire department and has not suffered as have many villages from the destructive element. At the first meeting of the village corporation in May, 1810, $100 were voted for the purchase of a fire engine, and a month later, it was ordered that twelve certain men be firemen, and that they be called out and exercised in using and examining the engine at least once a month, which should be on the last Saturday in each and every month; the time of meeting on said Saturday to be at sun two hours high in the afternoon until sunset. Non-attendance at the meetings without satisfactory excuse made the person so absenting himself liable to a fine of 50c and expulsion from the company. It was ordered "that within 90 days, every merchant and tavern-keeper in the village furnish himself with five leather fire buckets holding eight quarts and every other owner or occupant of any other house or building furnish himself with one bucket and that the owner of a bucket procure his name to be put on the same and that each and every owner of a bucket or buckets keep the same hung up near the outer door of the house or store and be appropriated to no other use except in case of fire and that every person neglecting or refusing to comply with this ordinance within the time limited shall be subject to a fine of twenty-five cents for each week thereafter for such neglect or refusal, to be collected as the law directs."

In 1812 the first engine house was built at a cost of $55. Four years later the fire company disbanded and the engine was sold for $15. In 1822, residents of the village were ordered to provide ladders long enough in each case to reach the roof of the dwelling; the engine house was sold at auction. In 1827, the first hooks and ladders were provided for at a cost of $20. In 1829 a new fire company was organized with thirteen members and a new engine. When this company disbanded in 1831, a new one was formed of eighteen members and in 1834 a $700 engine was purchased. In 1835, three sufficient reservoirs holding about 10,000 gallons each were constructed, as was an engine house at a cost of $92. Then a hook and ladder company was organized. In 1844 a second engine at a cost of $550 was purchased with hose and other appurtenances. In 1855 a school house was purchased for an engine house at a cost of $400. The Owahgena Fire Co. was first organized in 1862. Deluge Fire Co. was formed on the same date and a new engine purchased for $1,150. A steel fire bell costing $60 was mounted on the cupola of the engine house in 1863. Such a bell was not a matter of necessity, there being few fires, but it would serve many purposes. Alarms were also affixed to the bells of the Presbyterian and Methodist churches, with cord attachment. The present alarm is a horn blown by compressed air. Two additional reservoirs were constructed in 1873 near the Methodist church.

In 1874 it was "voted that active firemen shall henceforth be exempt from the poll tax." The next year, the fire, hook and ladder and hose companies disbanded and three new companies organized with a total membership of 86 members. Then the Owahgena Engine Co. No. 1 and Deluge Engine Co. No. 2 organized in 1877. Ledyard Hose Co. No. 1 organized in 1879. The equipment consisted of two hand engines, two hose carts and 1,000 feet of leather hose. The introduction of the village waterworks system in 1890 rendered the fire engines practically useless. The first chemical engine was purchased in 1920 at a cost of $2,500. This was found to be too small to be of much use in the country, so during the summer of 1925 a larger combination chemical engine and pump was purchased at a cost of nearly $6,000 raised mostly by public subscription. The fire department now consists of the Owahgena Hose Company and the Cazenovia Hook and Ladder Company.

Concerning military service, Mr. Forman wrote: "In the autumn of 1793 we were enrolled in Major Moses DeWitt's Battalion. He resided near James Ville in Manlius. We had orders to meet and choose officers for a company and to make our returns to him in order to obtain the military commissions. The following winter we went to Pompey Hill to receive our commissions. The first military duty by the Cazenovia Company was performed in the White Oak Grove at the foot of the lake. The next summer we were "warned to appear on lot No. 33 in Pompey Hollow, armed and equipped as the law directs for a Battalion training." Accordingly we met in the oaks at the appointed place well armed and equipped with good hickory clubs and a very few muskets. We formed and marched in military order as far as the swamp at the foot of the lake—this was the end of any road—here we halted and orders were given for every man to make the best of his way through the woods to the appointed ground and report himself to his Captain if he did not get lost in the woods. Some man observed that their little captain would get lost. The next training we were "ordered to appear armed and equipped as the law directs for a general review and inspection at Morehouse's Flat in Manlius." Gen. VanHorne was then the adjutant general of the state. This training closed all military connection with Onondaga County.

"The ensuing season, our population was so much augmented that we formed a separate Battalion in Cazenovia, John Lincklaen, Esq., Major

Commandant. I brought up from New York 112 complete stand of arms, bayonets and cartouch boxes; 77 light infantry hats, with silver eagles and L. I. Cyphers, all completely trimmed, and sold them at cost and charges. So we soon gained great laurels for our military prowess and received the applause of Adj. Gen. VanHorne. In due time as the population increased, a new brigade was formed in Madison County, Gen. Jonathan Forman, commanding—he was an old Revolutionary officer. This battalion now formed a regiment under Col. Lincklaen."

The military brigade was one of the great institutions of the early days. For the use of the militia when their headquarters were made in Cazenovia, a fine parade ground was laid out about 1810. This parade ground now "The Green" at the head of Hurd street, was much in the public eye and mind in those days and for many succeeding years. It was on this ground that the general training was held each year. Here they used to gather from all the contiguous country, the "Floodwood Militia," they were called, and there devote the day to military training under command of General Jabish Hurd. In early times, the Indians, it is said, were accustomed to gather in considerable numbers and with much interest watch the maneuvers of the men on the Green. On some occasions, it is said also, the Indians requested permission to join in the general training.

We were an important place in the War of 1812. War meetings were held; a company was raised here for the frontier. When several sturdy and patriotic Cazenovia citizens were called into active service, the Green was a school of military acting, and more, it was a school of military tragedy, for it trained men for war. On one occasion during this time a large troop of armed and equipped Indians passed through Cazenovia on their way to Sackett's Harbor to join the army in defense of their country. They camped for a little time on the old Green and then departed singing war songs as they went. Along in these days, too, the out-door shows that visited Cazenovia pitched their tents on the Green; many plays were staged. There was a certain character in town who had a most pronounced antipathy to all enterprises of this nature. This character was a colored woman who had positive notions on social economy, and she never hesitated to voice them. So when these show people gathered on the Green, she would go into their midst and there harangue them for a half hour at a time on the wickedness of their coming to town to take money from poor people. Not unlike those days, we now have the Redpath Chautauqua "show" which takes considerable money out of town but gives a fair educational return.

May 1861 saw the departure of twenty-four volunteers for the war. They were of Capt. Todd's Company. The inhabitants of the village gathered at the Lincklaen House corner to see the leave taking and bid farewell. When on the second of July, 1862, the President of the United States issued a call for three hundred thousand men to serve for three years, or during the war, the young men of the village and in the Seminary at once formed companies, and went through the manual of arms, drilling in the intervals of their work and studies. A war meeting was held on the night of July 26 for the purpose of providing suitable bounty and filling the quota of men from the town. The Free Church was crowded. Sufficient sums were subscribed to furnish a bounty of $25 to each recruit. Eleven volunteers enrolled their names that evening, and these formed the nucleus of Company K of the 114th Regiment. New Woodstock then added several hundred dollars to the bounty fund. Thursday, Aug. 14, 1862, was a day to be remembered. The inhabitants again gathered at the Lincklaen House corner while the company of 101 young men formed into line; prayer was offered, congratulations and leave taking of friends followed, and the procession moved off, amid the firing of guns and the ringing of bells to join the regiment at Norwich, where they were mustered into the United States' service. During the war, Cazenovia furnished 371 soldiers and 2 seamen. During the World War, 179 men from the town of Cazenovia answered the call to the colors. On Armistice Day, November 11, 1926, Cazenovia Post No. 88 of the American Legion, formally presented to the village a captured German 150 mm Howitzer, secured from the War Department as a war trophy. It is mounted on a concrete base on the south side of the public square, opposite the intersection of Sullivan with Albany street, pointing north. The artillery piece bears a bronze tablet placed on the base by the Legion, which reads:

"Presented to the Village of Cazenovia
by
Cazenovia Post No. 88
AMERICAN LEGION
In commemoration of those
who served from this community
In the Wars of The
United States."

There were three early burying-grounds—one over the hill from the West Shore Station, past the old golf links; one on the Burr farm on the west side of the lake, and one at the west end of the Green, either side of the First Presbyterian Church. The three present cemeteries are the Evergreen, or Protestant; the Catholic and the South Cemetery.

A nine hole golf course, "the sportiest and most scenic in the state," was opened in the spring of 1925 on the west side of the lake. The course on the Fairchild property, which had been in use many years, was abandoned at that time.

The citizens of the town were requested to meet at the Lincklaen

House in March, 1864, to take into consideration the propriety of taking measures for the construction of a horse railroad from the village to Chittenango Depot. "Such a road would be an advantage to the town—all kinds of business would be benefitted, real estate would advance in value; manufacturers would use the valuable water power now going to waste and the beautiful village would become a summer resort to many." However, the advantages of a horse railroad were not considered sufficient to pay for the outlay. A subscription paper was circulated and nearly funds enough pledged to defray the expense of the survey for a steam power road. In 1870 the Lehigh Valley R. R. was built to Canastota. It now runs between Elmira and Canastota. In 1872 the so-called Chenango Valley R. R., now a part of the New York Central property, was built to Syracuse. It runs between Earlville and Syracuse. Electric trains were put on the Lehigh the latter part of 1926. Auto bus service between Syracuse and points south and east of Cazenovia was inaugurated two or three years previously.

When Cazenovia was first settled, it belonged to the town of Whitestown. The way this singular occurrence happened, Whitestown once included all the county west to the military lands, and all new towns when set off, had their boundaries, so town meetings and elections had to be attended at Whitestown. In 1795 Cazenovia was erected into a Town—it comprised an area nearly equal to that of the whole of Madison County.

The first town meeting was held in April, 1795. Among the "rules and regulations" adopted on the occasion, was one—"that no man shall bring cattle into this town that does not belong to him to run at large on the commons, except working oxen and milk cows, on penalty of five pounds to the use of the town." One would suppose that a town of such dimensions, and only two years from the hand of nature, would have "commons" enough for all the cattle that could be brought on, unless their neighbors up the Missouri should drive on their buffaloes. Cazenovia was the first village incorporated in Madison County, the date of the act being February 7, 1810. The first corporation meeting was held in May, 1810.

From the time of the formation of the county to this date, Cazenovia had been looked upon as a suitable location for the county seat of the Courts of Justice, and had become so temporarily; consequently, the first criminal punished for murder in Madison County, was executed here. This was a wife poisoner, who had been confined in Whitestown jail, tried at a court held in a barn in the town of Sullivan, whence he was brought to Cazenovia and hung, the gallows being erected about half a mile east of the village. The county seat proper was located here in 1810, not, however, without some opposition from rival towns. A brick court-house was erected at a cost of upwards of $4,000 on the site where the Seminary Chapel now stands. The first courts were held here in 1812. The county seat was moved to Morrisville in 1817.

A "United States Telegraph" line was constructed between Chittenango and Cazenovia in October, 1865. Soon after, the Western Union brought a line in, and in a short time the two loops consolidated, in favor of the Western Union.

Previous to 1868, street lamps were installed, being kerosene lamps in a lantern-like arrangement on top of a post, at alternate corners. A note in the village paper says: "We are often met with the inquiry why our street lamps are not lighted on dark nights. We are informed that the wages of a person for lighting them are so comparatively high that the village fathers do not feel authorized to make the expense." A petition from the Chenango Street residents for light resulted in the lighting of the lamps again. The lamp-lighter was the delight and the target of the children, who pelted him with snow-balls in the winter and tipped his cart over in the summer. Even grown-ups were known to "borrow" his chimneys. The electric light system was installed in 1898.

The village, feeling the necessity of a place nearer than Morrisville for the safe-keeping of those who imbibed too freely, voted $600 in 1869 for a lock-up.

The Cazenovia Band was organized in 1852. A band stand was erected in the square in front of the Cazenovia House in 1873. Succeeding years produced bands of more or less merit until about 1926 when the bandstand was torn down.

The first telephones were installed in 1895.

In 1803, the census of the village was 100 inhabitants. The state census of 1925 recorded 1686 inhabitants.

Last, but not least, the town clock marks time with the historian. It is one of those things which is taken for granted, its origin never questioned. The clock in the Seminary tower and in the Presbyterian Church tower gave up the struggle long ago, but the town clock goes on forever.

The earliest record of the clock is contained in an editorial of the Cazenovia Republican of November 5, 1862, which reads: "The old town clock, which for so many years has graced the spire of the Methodist church, is a wreck. It is so badly damaged that repairs are impossible and it is better to put up a new and reliable clock than to attempt to patch up an old and worthless one. The old clock is the first iron town clock (and the only one of that pattern) built by Mr. Jehiel Clark. It was never a very good one, but by the expenditure of a good deal of money and trouble it has been made to do useful service for about twenty years. The question of replacing it by another will be voted on at the coming charter election. Our people have too long enjoyed the benefits and conveniences.

of a town clock to consent to be without one now. It is certain that it will be voted to buy one, but the question is, what one? Mr. J. W. Marshall has one of the handsomest clocks ever made, built on a contract for a thousand dollar clock. It is jeweled throughout and well worth the thousand dollars originally asked for it. This splendid clock Mr. Marshall offers to put up and keep in running order one year for $500. It is not likely that we shall ever have another opportunity to get such a clock for so little money. It was built by Mr. Marshall for the late Mr. A. W. Van Riper, who had so much confidence in its accuracy as a time-keeper that he offered to give it to the village if on trial it should vary fifteen minutes within a year. Mr. Marshall will do the same if it is preferred to his other offer Town clocks can be bought more cheaply than this. Mr. Marshall has them for sale, but they are much dearer at the price charged for them than is the large clock. The cheap ones will not last so long and will not keep so good time while they do last. Mr. Marshall's clock can be seen by those interested at his shop, and we have a large engraving of it which we shall be happy to show. Voters within the corporate limits of Cazenovia ought to inform themselves on this subject, as it will come up for decision at the charter election to be held next month."

Two weeks later the paper carried this editorial: "Citizens of this corporation should be making up their minds as to how they will vote on the town clock question. Mr. Marshall's clock is up and noting the time accurately. It is a beautiful piece of workmanship, of brass, highly finished, the pivot-holes and verge pallets jeweled, and, in brief, the clock is provided with every improvement that experience and ingenuity can suggest. There is some opposition to the purchase of this clock, because an iron one can be bought for less money. Undoubtedly an iron clock might be bought that would keep time well for a few years, but it is unreasonable to suppose that an iron or steel surface will withstand friction as long as a jeweled one. The result with the iron clock would be that within a few years we should have just such an unreliable time-keeper as the old clock was, and after expending two or three hundred dollars for repairs and attendance, we should have to throw away the iron machine and pay a thousand dollars to replace it with just such a clock as we have now offered to us for $500. It is always bad policy to buy an inferior article because it is cheap!"

At the election on December 2, 1862, by a resolution, the trustees were authorized to hire the clock for a year and to call a special meeting to purchase it during the year if deemed by them proper. Records show that $50 rent for the clock was paid in 1866 and again in 1868. It is possible that $50 a year was paid from 1862 until 1870 when the clock was bought for $400. It had been placed in the tower of the First Methodist church. When the new church was built, a meeting of the electors was called to vote on the proposition that $1,000 be raised by tax to be paid for the permanent use of a tower in which to place the clock, and that $250 be raised to pay for necessary fixtures and the expense of placing the clock in the tower. Both of these propositions were defeated. Then at a meeting of the Trustees of the Methodist church, the following preamble and resolution were adopted, viz: "Whereas, All negotiations between this Board and the citizens and trustees of the village in relation to the town clock have failed to secure to us any aid in erecting a suitable tower for the clock, therefore, Resolved, That we do hereby grant permission to the trustees of the village to place the town clock in the tower of our new church without compensation." At a meeting two weeks later of the Board of Trustees of the village, on motion of G. H. Atwell, it was unanimously resolved that the offer made by the Trustees of the First M. E. Church tendering to the village the use of the tower of said Church in which to place the village clock, without compensation, be gratefully accepted. Two hundred and thirty dollars was to be raised by tax to pay the expenses incurred in placing the clock in the tower of the M. E. Church where it has been since 1874. The face of the clock, on the outside of the tower, is above the bell which in turn is above the clock machinery. The pendulum of the clock hangs 18 feet long; it is a wooden stick with a lead disc about 1 foot in diameter on the end. The striking weight weighs 2400 pounds and is hung by a cable; the weight that runs the clock weighs 1400 pounds and is hung by a rope. The hands are turned by a wooden stick about an inch square and about 30 feet long. The clock is wound once a week but would run two or three days longer. The bell which was in the first church, was put in the new church and has served as church bell and to strike the hours of the clock. "The town clock regulates the sun."

RELIGION

CHAPTER V.

Religion

The itinerant preacher followed hard after the pioneer. From the east, through the Mohawk Valley, and from the south, along the Susquehanna and its tributaries, they entered and traversed the territory. Over the obscure and difficult forest paths, across the unbridged streams, around the impracticable morass, through the summer rains and the winter snows, with a pittance for a salary, and often with scanty food and clothing, they sought the scattered homes of the frontier "to gather the outcasts and to seek the lost." What this fair region of central and western New York owes to the labor and sacrifices of that heroic band no mortal can estimate. The computation must include more than appears in the Societies and Churches which they founded. Their influence has penetrated all society, their fruits are found in all the churches.

Those who settled this region of country were a religious people, who brought with them a love of religious institutions and the religious observances to which they had been accustomed in their Holland and New England homes, hence, soon after the azure blue of heaven's high dome became visible through the first clearings in the dense forest wilderness which surrounded their rude habitations, devout thanksgivings ascended to the power which had preserved them from past dangers and a continuance of that merciful protection fervently invoked in public gatherings of their numbers; and within six years from the time the first habitation was planted in these wilds as the herald of an on-coming civilization, we find them an organized band for the more effective prosecution of their religious plans and purposes.

The first church was the Presbyterian. When it was built it was the first church west of Albany. It is recorded that at a meeting held at the schoolhouse near the lake, in November, 1798, six men were elected to be "The Trustees of the First Presbyterian congregation of the town of Cazenovia." There was then neither minister, elder nor deacon. At the first meeting of the trustees, it was resolved to circulate a subscription paper for the support of preaching, the subscriptions to which were to be paid either in cash or produce at John Lincklaen's mill near the lake. Two hundred and ninety-three dollars was subscribed. Rev. Joshua Leonard was invited "to tarry with us awhile and preach." It was agreed to allow him "$6 per Sabbath and pay all his expenses of board and horse-keeping provided he does not settle with us." Up to April, 1799, preaching was held at different places, the place of meeting being designated by the congregation, and the inconvenience attending that practice made it desirable to settle a pastor and establish meetings regularly at one place. Accordingly it was decided to circulate another subscription paper for the purpose of supporting a settled minister to preach regularly every Sabbath at the schoolhouse.

In May, 1799, a church of the Presbyterian order, composed of eight members, was organized under the ministrations of Rev. Leonard, known as "Priest Leonard," who was engaged as pastor at a salary of $300 per year. At the close of the installation exercises the congregation elected trustees and instructed them to make a pulpit and seats in the schoolhouse which stood just across the outlet bridge where the street runs toward the West Shore railroad station. Here they worshipped until they built a church edifice which was dedicated on February 14, 1806.

The cost of the building is not known, but the pews were sold at public auction for more than $5,000. Some persons bought two or three or more. They paid large sums considering their means and were willing to submit to inconveniences that they might establish the worship of God. Col. Lincklaen purchased three dozen of Psalm books; Mrs. Lincklaen furnished the ornaments for the pulpit; Mrs. Forman gave a Bible and hymn book for the pulpit, at a cost of nearly $30.* The town was then thinly settled; the people mostly lived in log houses situated in the woods, and generally had not paid for their land. Yet within less than seven years from the organization of the church, it had expended $8,000 for religious purposes. Communion was denied those who refused to contribute a just and equal part and proportion toward defraying the common expenses of the church.

The first church building, erected on the site of the present Emory estate on the Green, was a very cold place in the winter. It was not the practice then to have fire in the church except in the little foot stoves which the ladies used to take with them, but they introduced an improvement by putting two stoves under the gallery, near the door, with pipes running to a large sheet iron drum in the center of the church, elevated considerably above the heads of the congregation and a pipe leading from the drum to the outside of the church. It did not add very much to the good appearance of the church, but it was much more comfortable. There was a gallery all around and a sounding board over the high pulpit. It seemed to be the fashion then to get the minister as far from the people as possible. There was a liberal sprinkling of the sturdy Scotch element among the Presbyterians. The church kept a watchful eye on its members. Here one came and confessed to too free use of wine and another to taking

---

*One writer says one "could read inscribed in a large bold handwriting in the pulpit Bible, that it was a gift to the church from Mr. Lincklaen, who was a regular attendant and liberal supporter of the church."

illegal interest; others were labored with and brought before the church, one for talking business on Sunday, another for dishonest deal, and a sister for gossiping. Several lay members were tried for heresy; letters were refused to members going to other denominations, they being labeled on the records "Covenant breaker," "Gone to the Baptists" or "Gone to the Methodists." The Society adopted as a seal the device of a pigeon bearing an olive branch.

A parsonage was built in 1816 at a cost of about $1,000. Finding the location of the church inconvenient, the building was removed, down Hurd Street, to its present site in the summer of 1828. The bell was securely tied in the belfry to keep it quiet during the moving process. The building was thoroughly repaired and altered to suit the time and occupied without material change until 1834, when improvements were made costing nearly $800. The session house, or chapel, connected with the church, was built in 1854. Alterations were made in the Spring of 1868 costing $9,000, the furnishings about $3,000 more. The galleries on three sides were removed, leaving but the one for the organ and singers. A new clock, with the words "Redeeming The Time" on its face, was installed as the gift of Dr. Rogers of Brooklyn. Rededication services were in December, 1869. The organ, costing $2,250, was installed in 1870 as the gift of Mr. and Mrs. B. R. Wendell. A new parsonage costing about $5,000 was erected in 1870. As a memorial to Mr. Burr Wendell, his wife and daughter had the interior of the church newly decorated in 1914.

The Baptists organized almost simultaneously with the Presbyterians. Among the Baptists who settled near the site of New Woodstock, were a number of active, zealous young men from Woodstock, Conn. In 1800 Elder James Bacon came on from Torrington, Mass., and through his efforts a church was organized the following year. On the 18th day of March, 1801, a little band of ten met, but six others were baptized that spring and the sixteen were fellowshipped June 17, 1801. A small log meeting house was built by this society in 1802 which was occupied until a few years later when the church united with the Presbyterians in building a frame edifice. This was soon outgrown and in 1815 the present building was erected. (In New Woodstock).

The Baptist Church in Cazenovia village was formed as a result of meetings held in 1803 in the school house two miles south of the village ("Perkins' District") and conducted by Elder Bacon. Other elders conducted the meetings there until 1813, when they were held in the court house in the village until 1817. In that year the foundations of a meeting house were laid and in the following year it was in condition for occupancy. On September 6, 1820, thirty-six male and fifty-five female members were dismissed from the Baptist church of New Woodstock and a separate organization was effected in Cazenovia. The Sunday school was opened in 1823. In 1835 the church was repaired and improved and again in 1868. It was rededicated on January 14, 1869. The church edifice was burned to the ground in 1871, but regular appointments were maintained in an adjoining hall. The society rebuilt with brick at a cost of $15,200 and in June, 1880, reported the new edifice paid for and dedicated. The organ was installed in 1872. The kitchen was added about 1908. In 1916 the interior of the church was newly decorated; a hardwood floor was laid in the lecture room and a new carpet laid in the auditorium. During the summer of 1927, a hardwood floor was laid in the auditorium and the walls were re-decorated. The ordinance of baptism was administered in the lake for many years. Evening services in the early days were called at "early candlelighting." At the time the meetings were transferred from the school house to the court house, the only Baptists living in the village were "two females, both poor, and having intemperate husbands." The salary a hundred years ago was $350, in quarterly payments, one half in cash and the remainder in produce at cash prices, likewise the use of the parsonage. The first Baptist Missionary Society in America was formed in Cazenovia.

No records of the Methodist Church prior to its incorporation have been preserved, hence we are unable to definitely trace its history during the succeeding interval. One writer states:

"At the early date which marks the beginning of this history, Cazenovia and all the territory lying west in the state of New York was embraced in the bounds of the Genesee Conference. Cazenovia was a weak point in Methodism, on a six weeks' circuit, having no church edifice within its limits save the old Court-house in Cazenovia village. There were only five or six Methodist families in the place. The courts had been removed to Morrisville, and the Court-house was for sale. There was a sharp competition between the Baptist minister and the Methodists for the possession of the house. It was to be sold on a given day, and each party intended to secure the prize. However, the Methodists, having bid the highest sum, $1,810, and given a reliable bond for its payment, were put into immediate possession of the premises. This was in 1818. After a time, the trustees of the Cazenovia Methodist Society, who were personally responsible, found themselves embarrassed by the debt on the Court-house, so they petitioned the Conference for relief, with the result that it was taken over for the Seminary."

Another writer states: "In 1816 the Cortland circuit was formed and Cazenovia was included in it. The preacher formed a small class in the village, consisting mostly of young people, who were zealous and united. One member was a man of some means; the remainder of the class were poor, a majority of them single persons. The church was incorporated in

1830; a subscription was soon started to obtain funds with which to build a chapel, the supscriptions not to be binding unless $3,000 or more was subscribed. As only a little less than $2,000 was pledged by nineteen individuals, the project was abandoned. On January 25, 1832, it was resolved to raise a fund by selling the pews of a contemplated church to be built on the corner lot south of the Seminary, of brick or stone. The sales of pews continued at a few intervals until January, 1833, at which time little more than $4,000 had been realized. $3,000 additional were borrowed. In the spring of that year work on the building was begun and it was finished during the year. This building was used until 1873, when the present fine edifice was completed at a cost, with furnishings, of about $39,000."

Although it was in the year 1825 when a "station" was formed in Cazenovia village, a small class had existed, supplied by circuit preachers who rode through the country on horseback and sometimes received for their year's work as much as $75 including donations. Their expenditures usually exceeded their receipts, as they had to pay the expenses of themselves and equipage. When the Seminary was started in December, 1824, preaching services were held in the chapel Sabbath morning, the lack of labor from the circuit preachers being supplied chiefly by Principal Porter until the Conference of 1825, when a station preacher was appointed. When the "Stone Church" was completed, it was equal if not superior to any edifice of the kind in the Conference at the time. The church was presented with a house and lot for a parsonage in December, 1870, valued at $2,000.

Still another writer says: "Methodism in Cazenovia dates from 1816, in which year a class meeting was formed and met in a building once used as a distillery. This class existed as such until 1824, when it was re-organized, becoming the First Methodist Episcopal Church, the members worshipping for a time in the Madison County Court House. After much difficulty and sacrifice the first church building, constructed of stone, was dedicated in the year 1833. In time this structure became inadequate and plans were made for the building of a new and larger church. After a long struggle the present edifice, built and furnished at a cost of $35,000 was dedicated December 17, 1873. Rather extensive repairs were made to the building in 1900. The recent repairs and improvements in the property made in 1924, have made the church attractive and convenient."

At the time of the recent repairs and improvements, the whole interior was redecorated, new electric fixtures were placed throughout, a new roof was put on, the stained windows were repaired, the dining room was enlarged, the kitchen refurnished including new dishes, and an expensive heating plant was installed. The entire cost was estimated as $15,000.

On November 4, 1844, twelve men met in the room occupied as the high school room, on the public square, where they were accustomed to celebrate divine worship according to the rites of the Protestant Episcopal church, for the purpose of incorporating themselves as a religious society. Rev. Gallagher, who was then a missionary at this place, having preached here for the first time in September, in the chapel of the Seminary, was called to the chair. It was decided to incorporate under the name of "The Rector, Wardens and Vestrymen of St. Peter's church in the town of Cazenovia, in the County of Madison." Two wardens were elected and eight vestrymen. December 1, 1844, the congregation worshipped for the first time in the school room which had been fitted up neatly and comfortably at an expense of about $200. Previous to the organization, services had been held here by two Bishops and thirteen ministers. Owing to an informality in the proceedings, the parish was not received into union with the Convention in 1845. It was subsequently re-organized and admitted the following year. Rev. Gallagher, who had officiated as rector since the organization, severed his connection with the parish in 1846. Lay reading was statedly held for several months. In 1847 a site for a church was selected. The church was finished and consecrated in 1848. A pastor was called at a salary of $300 per year and such additional sum as could be raised for his support.

About 1900 the transept was added. In 1924-25 the old guild room and the kitchen were remodeled and redecorated. This work was done at the direction of Mrs. Fairchild as a memorial to her husband, the Hon. Charles S. Fairchild. After thirty-five years' pastorate, the Rev. John T. Rose resigned the rectorship of St. Peters' January 1, 1927. As a token of esteem he was presented with a purse of $4,000 by his congregation and friends who had been associated with the church during his pastorate.

St. James' Roman Catholic Church was organized in 1849 by Rev. Hayes of Syracuse, who had previously conducted meetings in private houses at intervals for some six months. The first Mass said near Cazenovia was celebrated at a home in Shelter Valley about the year 1844. The present brick church edifice was erected in 1849-50. The first services were held in the church in May, 1850, before the pews were put in. The church was not entirely completed until 1852; it was dedicated June 26, 1854. Its cost was about $5,000. In 1862, it was enlarged and improved at a cost of $4,500.

Services were conducted in the church before its completion by Rev. Hayes and three assistants until the first resident pastor was appointed in 1853. The out-missions then were Pompey Hill, Truxton and Chittenango. A parsonage was purchased in 1860 for $1,250, and a cemetery, embracing a little more than two acres, was bought in 1861 for $200. Gen. J. D. Ledyard and his son, Ledyard Lincklaen, were liberal contributors to the funds for the purchase of the cemetery, and to the church improvements made in 1862. They were the principal donors of two stained-glass windows which embellish the church. The present rectory was built in 1896. In 1913 many improvements were made: a new vestibule was built and an addition at the rear of the church. In 1916 new altars were added. The combined cost of this work was in the neighborhood of $25,000. Work was started in the spring of 1928 on an assembly and recreational building as a place in which to hold the church suppers, Christmas festivities, social and recreational sports.

In 1833 a Free Church was organized largely from the Presbyterians who split on the subject of abolition. A good deal of bitterness existed on both sides for some years, but the free church ceased to exist before the war. An abolition convention was held here about 1847.

In 1841 a number of members left the Presbyterian society and formed the First Congregational Church, which built and worshipped in what became Concert Hall. This was also called the Free Church and the Abolitionist Church. It at once entered upon a stormy and strenuous career. It was in a sense a free lance in creeds and Christianity, because, with the adherents of this church, true Christianity involved a principle, that of anti-slavery. There were many turbulent meetings between the pro and anti-slavery elements. Rev. John Ingersoll, father of Col. Robert G. Ingersoll, the famous agnostic, was one of the preachers.

In the early fifties a Universalist Society had a church in the village. It had considerable numerical strength for a little time. It soon dwindled, however, and so in a few years disorganized and ceased to exist altogether. The building still stands at Williams Street corner and has been used for a skating rink and for stores.

There was once a grove at the head of the lake which was a favorite picnic ground and popular for fishing parties. Refreshments for man and beast; boats, fishing tackle, bait, etc., were furnished. At that time camp meetings had become a prominent though extra means of grace in the Methodist Church. The Lake View Camp Meeting Association was formed to purchase and beautify the picnic grounds for camp meetings. During the first camp meeting, between fifty and sixty tents were pitched where many families were domiciled. The tents formed the outside of a circle, the interior of which was fitted up with seats and a speaker's stand. People came from all the surrounding country; railroads reduced their fares, a steamer and a barge were put on the lake to convey the people from the station to the head of the lake. Between five and eight thousand people and more than a thousand teams were on the grounds the first Sunday although neither the trains nor boats ran on Sundays, keeping an undesirable element away. Religious services were held almost continuously, mostly in the open space, but sometimes in the tents. The Methodists of the Syracuse district joined those of the Cazenovia district.

EDUCATION

Chapter VI.

Education

Historically, the church has always been the sworn and unfaltering ally of education. After the third century, wherever the church was planted, the elementary instruction of the poor began. By the side of the church rose the school house. The church school was the forerunner of the public free schools.

The early school buildings, like the homes of the children, were generally log structures. The windows were small and few in number, the otherwise deficient light being supplied by the capacious chimneys, and by crevices in the walls and roof. On dark days the pupils were arranged about the base of the large chimney, to utilize the light which poured down its throat, and without which, study would have been impossible. The floor and ceiling, when such were provided, consisted of loose, rough boards, through the joints of which the wind had a free circulation, affording ofttimes a superabundance of fresh air. The seats were without backs, and were often formed of rived portions of forest trees, or, where saw-mills existed, of planks or slabs, supported at either end by roughly formed and acute-angled legs, which would often seek in vain for a secure rest upon the uneven floor. From such seats, sufficiently high for adults, dangled for six tedious hours daily, the uneasy limbs of children from four to six years of age, with no support for either legs, arms or backs; and there they must cling, and keep quiet, under penalty of a blow from the whip or ferrule of the teacher. When weary, and they often became so, sleep overtook not only their limbs, in which the circulation was impeded by the sharp-angled seats, but also their entire bodies, and a careless tilt of the unsteady seat precipitated the sleepers to the floor.

But the broad open fire-places of those primitive schoolrooms were objects of the highest interest. It was not alone the light which they supplied; they were miniature bonfires, on which the otherwise undelighted eyes of the pupils rested with pleasure. They gorged, at once, and without crowding, a full quarter of a cord of wood, and, when in full blast, glowed like the log heaps of the settlers' fallow ground. Around the blazing pile the pupils on entering arranged themselves, and by repeated turnings, at length so saturated with warmth their thick, home-made clothing, as, for a short time, to be comfortable upon their seats. Then and for some years later, books of any kind, except the Bible, hymn book and almanac, were a luxury rarely seen in the homes of the people. School books were very few, and confined to the three subjects of reading, spelling and arithmetic; the latter for the boys in all cases, but not always for the girls, who, it was thought, were sufficiently educated if they could read and write. The first school books were of English production and had been generally used in New England. Many of them found their way into the early schools of these counties, having descended to the children from the parents who had used them.

The early school discipline was but a counterpart of the prevailing errors of the time. It was mainly physical. The whip and the ferrule were as constant companions of the teacher as the book or the pen, and were equally intended for use. A goodly store of well-seasoned switches was always ready for extra occasions. The whip fell frequently upon the mischievous and idle without warning or explanation, but with young pupils, the whip was supplemented by many ingenious yet cruel devices, such as a gag in the mouth; standing on one foot holding an object in the extended or uplifted hand; resting one hand and one foot upon the floor, or holding a heavy weight in both hands, the body inclined forward. These and many other cruel tortures were regularly practiced for more than a generation to incite in children the love of order, of books and of schools.

One of the fundamentals of the early Cazenovia settlers' creed was education. Their ideals of life were high and education was the foundation on which to build and sustain their ideals. Early in 1796 a school had been established in the settlement. Finally as the village grew, new schools were established until there were three located in different sections of the village. One was on the site of the present Presbyterian parsonage.

The first school in Cazenovia was kept in a building which stood south of the west bridge, near the corner of Ledyard Avenue and Rippleton Road. When the law of 1805 was passed, organizing the common school system, the inhabitants united in an agreement to erect a commodious school house. Three hundred and forty-five dollars were to be raised in shares of $15 each, one-third in wheat, one-third in corn, and one-third in cash. During the year 1813 school districts were organized and in 1814 the school houses were erected.

The first appropriation of public school money was made to Cazenovia in 1816, $193.56 being granted. A law was passed in 1853 providing for union free schools. In 1875, the three school districts were united to form the Cazenovia Union School. The site of the schoolhouse in one district was selected as the site of the new schoolhouse for the Union School, while the schoolhouses and lots in the other two districts were directed to be sold. In 1878 one of the unsold school buildings was moved to the lot on Sullivan street, placed in the rear of the schoolhouse already there, and fitted for use, to give needed increased accommodation. These buildings were replaced by a much larger building in 1901. In the summer of 1924, the state board recommended a new, larger building and in the summer of

1925, the same site was selected. In 1926 more ground was bought and in 1927 preparations were begun for a larger building.

Several select schools have been factors in the educational affairs of the village. A high school was once started in opposition to the Seminary. There have also been splendid kindergartens at various times.

An elementary education was a privilege which, if enjoyed, must be paid for by the individual. Now, it is a duty, imposed, provided for and enforced by the state. The object of education is the gaining of intellectual and moral power.

CAZENOVIA SEMINARY

The credit, with good reason, has generally been awarded to George Gary as the most prominent instrument in getting the Seminary in operation as an accomplished fact; but it is not so generally known that the first steps which led to this result were taken under the advice and direction of Mr. Charles Giles, while presiding elder of the district which embraced the village of Cazenovia. It is true the enterprise thus inaugurated, by reason of various delays and embarrassments, was by no means fully effected when he left the district; still, great credit is due Mr. Giles for the deep interest he took in the matter, and the progress made when Mr. Gary became a resident of Cazenovia.

Mr. Giles stated in his autobiography: "At this time our Conference was in a prosperous condition, exerting a happy influence on the community by its efficient ministry. The sphere for usefulness was widening around us, and hence our obligations were pressing us forward. The public mind began to be excited by a laudable spirit of enterprise; improvements in many things were being inaugurated; and literature was on the advance, and receiving encouragement everywhere. At this favorable juncture I was fully convinced that the time had come for our Conference to engage in a public literary enterprise. Learning being an auxiliary to religon in every department of the church, we, therefore, greatly needed a literary institution under the supervision and patronage of the Conference. I, therefore, engaged in the undertaking, with high expectations that in a few passing years a flourishing seminary of learning would be seen as an ornamental appendage to our village.

"As a proper preliminary measure a village meeting was called to give character and publicity to our object and to elicit the views and opinions of the citizens respecting the contemplated design. According to our expectations a respectable number of influential gentlemen attended the meeting. In the address an attempt was made to show the profitable advantages the village would derive from a literary establishment there. Many of the attendants were delighted with the scheme; such an institution as was in contemplation would more than compensate for the loss they had sustained by the removal of the county seat. Besides, they confessed they needed some public enterprise to give a spur to business, and to resuscitate the village which was then in a languishing condition.

"After doing all that could be done to give form and tangibility to the design, I carried it up to the next annual Conference which passed a resolution sanctioning the design."

As early as 1819 the anxious eyes of many friends of education and religion had been fixed upon Cazenovia as the appropriate location for a Conference Seminary, although some Central New York Methodists preferred Ithaca for the site, so it was not an accident that George Gary was appointed presiding elder for Chenango District in 1823 and that Cazenovia was selected as his place of residence. The first "Conference Seminary in the Methodist Episcopal Church" was established at Newmarket, N. H., in 1817. It continued in existence only to 1825. Cazenovia was the second seminary in the United States under the control of the Methodist Episcopal Church.

When the county seat was moved from Cazenovia to Morrisville, the court house was sold to a group of Methodists who later found themselves unable to pay for it and petitioned the Conference for relief, so it was decided by the conference to take the building and fit it up for occupancy by the school.

It was "Resolved, That any person contributing one hundred dollars to the funds of the institution should be entitled to send one scholar for four years free of charge, provided that he reside within five miles of the Seminary." The terms were specified; the year was divided into quarters and each quarter was to continue eleven weeks. A vacation of two weeks was to follow each quarter. The tuition for the first two classes was to cost $4 per quarter; for the third class, $3 and for the fourth class $2.50. Rev. Nathaniel Porter was secured as principal and the Seminary was opened, a beginning marked by rivalry, embarrassments, sacrifice and success.

The institution opened on December 1, 1824, under the name "The Seminary of the Genesee Conference." When the bell rang its first call, eight pupils responded. Rev. Porter was greatly astonished to find that it was proposed to establish a Conference seminary in a place where there was next to no Methodist Society, there being at that time only one family in the village which represented this denomination besides that of Presiding Elder Gary. Aware of the absurdity of expecting to build up a vigorous, influential, and enduring Methodist academy in a village where there was no Methodist church, he clearly saw he had a double enterprise before him. Hence he at once established preaching every Sunday morning in the chapel; the service to be conducted by himself, assisted by circuit preachers;

at the same time encouraging all his pupils at other hours to attend the Presbyterian church, the only place where public preaching had been statedly sustained.

The school term had not continued more than five weeks before the number of students had increased to more than fifty. At the end of the year, one hundred and twenty-one had registered. At the beginning, the school was designed for males only, but at some time during the first term girls were admitted. Co-education was then in full operation and excited neither opposition nor comment. The young ladies lived in a separate building but both sexes took their meals at the same tables, pursued substantially the same studies and recited in the same classes.

In 1826 the numbers had so increased, the building was too small, so the first building next west of the court house (now Eddy Hall) was erected and occupied as a boarding hall. The dining hall was opened in the basement of this building in 1828. There were outside entrances, either side of the front steps. About one-half of the students boarded and lodged in the Hall, but most of the old students roomed elsewhere. It was surprising how many occupied cells (for they could hardly be called rooms) in the then contracted dimensions of the two buildings. Indeed, so small were the gentlemen's rooms in the new building that ordinary bedsteads were out of the question. Instead, there were turn-up bedsteads which when folded served as a wardrobe as well as a sleeping apparatus; but so limited was the space that the couches were both too narrow and too thin for the accommodation of two students comfortably. In June, 1829, it was "Resolved, That the price of board in the hall be raised to one dollar per week after the close of the present term." That same year at a meeting of the trustees, it was "Resolved, That any person subscribing and securing to the funds of the institution the sum of $1,000 shall have the privilege of educating one scholar free from the expense of tuition so long as the institution shall exist."

The trustees appointed a committee in 1831 to establish a library, and to examine a certain circulating library. These steps must have been to some extent successful, since very soon thereafter it was resolved to charge students twelve and a half cents per quarter for the use of the library. A reading room was fitted up and the publishing of a paper considered. Here also, began a policy of granting free tuition, under limitations, to ministers.

The demand for additional room for the wants of the school began to be felt in 1832, so measures were taken to erect a building to the west of Eddy Hall. Subscriptions were solicited in the village. A sum of $3,000 was borrowed. The result of these steps was a resolution to erect two additional buildings, one of brick, three stories high for a Gentlemen's hall, and one of wood, two stories high. The wooden building was built at the rear of the brick building and was used for a new dining hall on the first floor, and a women's dormitory on the second floor. The ladies who roomed on the west side of the building, had a commanding view of the sheds in the rear of the Baptist Church, but this was not unfavorable to study, for some of the best students of those times roomed and studied there.

In the earlier stage of the Seminary's history, the primary department was reckoned as part of the institution. There was a "Preceptor of the juvenile male" and a "Preceptress of the juvenile female department," but as the school rose in rank, and the standard was elevated, this department was discontinued. The music department was inaugurated at the Winter term of 1835.

The rules of the Seminary were rigid and some of them were considered tyrannical. Prayers at five o'clock in the morning and evening; recess and breakfast from seven to eight; noon recess and dinner from twelve to one; afternoon recess from five to seven, and the rest of the time, study and sleep. But, although idleness was a great sin, and strenuously to be guarded against, the mortal sin, toward which the ladies and gentlemen were continually suspected of a leaning, was a hankering after each other's society. True, they worshipped together, recited together, and ate at the same tables, but they were not to talk together. Occasional social gatherings of the students and teachers, called "Parties" had been allowed but were frowned upon by some of the trustees as exerting a bad influence on the piety and religious convictions of the students, engendering too much trifling, hindering revivals and the expense of a shilling apiece for those who attended was too much. Although the above are by no means all the rules which some thought were severe, let us look a little more closely into the import of some of them. To begin: Prayers at five in the morning, as well as evening, summer and winter. Only think of it! All the students, male and female, in order to keep a good standing, were required to be in their seats for morning worship at five o'clock, which in the winter means two hours before daylight. There was no internal access to the chapel in those days for the ladies from their hall. They came in shivering, wrapped in cloaks that extended from the crowns of their heads almost to their feet. The interval between prayers and the breakfast bell was spent chiefly in bed-making, room-sweeping, (mopping was done on Saturday after public declamations in the chapel—carpets being as rare as angels' visits) and putting the outer man to rights for a decent appearance at the long, narrow dining table, which was covered with oilcloth—the gentlemen seated on small backless stools on one side and the ladies on the other. The table furniture was correspondingly plain. The knives were not silver plated, and the forks had only two tines, but they answered the purpose tolerably well. The fare, though not luxurious, was wholesome, abundant and gave general satisfaction. There were many flirtations, and not a few attachments and engagements, some of which terminated in marriage. There were disappointments, jealousies, and heart-burning; but, on the whole, what with walking, driving and sailing on the lake, there was no lack of recreation, and life at Cazenovia was pleasant.

After the terms of the school had been arranged for two sessions of twenty-two weeks each, it was found there was a tendency to a decreased attendance near the close of the sessions. This led to a change to three terms of fifteen weeks each. A three years' course of study was adopted in 1839 on the completion of which diplomas were conferred. It is believed this was the first graduating course adopted by any Seminary in the State. The Seminary then ranked as tenth in the state, as measured by numbers of students and public moneys, but it stood first between the years 1872 and 1875. The first class graduating in the three years' course was in 1841.

The need of better accommodations for the school had long been seen and painfully felt. At a meeting of the board in 1851 it was "Resolved, That a subscription be drawn to raise $6,000 for that purpose." Six thousand one hundred dollars of the money secured by subscription was raised in Cazenovia, and Williams Hall was completed in 1853. General Jonathan D. Ledyard, together with his sons, gave one-third of what was required to build Williams Hall, and to put the chapel building in condition. He also gave $600 for an organ.

In 1853, Mr. B. R. Wendell established a gold medal prize to be awarded to the best scholar during the entire year, taking into account general character, punctuality, deportment and scholarly attainments. This was the initiation of the policy of awarding prizes, which has grown to be general in the school.

In the early fifties the Seminary had as a student a young Indian, said to be the son of a once famous Onondaga chief whose name was A-ta-her-ho. It is said also that this A-ta-her-ho was a mighty power in the Iroquois League in their days of life and activity. The Indian student became a physician of considerable note in New York City.

During the period between 1857 and 1862 the wants of the Seminary were of a most pressing character, especially as to improvements in the buidings and increased facilities. The finances of the board were not inspiring, the changes in the faculty were quite numerous and attended with not a little perplexity. Changes also in the board of trustees were not unimportant. During this period, also, the war broke out and the school was heavily drawn upon by the necessities of the nation to subdue armed rebellion. Prices were greatly augmented. It was necessary to raise the price of board; the wisdom and enterprise of the friends of the Seminary were taxed to the uttermost. Some students found fault at being obliged to pay the enormous sum of one dollar sixty-two and one-half cents per week! while all they legitimately received for the same in return was board, lodging, washing, fuel, lights, and, if sick, the best of care! Can it be wondered the school suffered financial embarrassment when it is remembered that previous to 1829 the price of board in the hall was less than one dollar per week?

The closing weeks of the 1862 academic year and the vacation which immediately followed were days of darkness, of excitement, and of loyal patriotism in all the land. It is claimed, on behalf of the Seminary, that she furnished the nucleus and gave the momentum which sent to the field one of the best companies of the noble One Hundred and Fourteenth Regiment, which made such an honorable record during the war. The "Girl I Left Behind Me Society" came into being at this time and was active in sending remembrances to the student soldiers.

In 1863 a public meeting was called in relation to the contemplated improvements of the Seminary buildings and grounds. It was deemed impossible to suitably repair the west building, so plans were made for a new building on the ground of the old one, with an extension to the north. It was proposed to raise $20,000 for buildings, Cazenovia to raise $5,000 of the amount. When little more than half the fund had been raised, work was commenced and proceeded until the front building was erected, when it was discovered the funds were not sufficient to complete the rear building. Great difficulty was experienced during the winter term of 1864 in finding boarding places for the students. An extensive boarding house for them in the village would have been a paying institution. It was especially desired that the ladies board out.

The building work was postponed until the demands of the Seminary were such that in 1870 the trustees were compelled to devise means with which to complete the enterprise. Bonds for $30,000 were issued and after many difficulties and struggles, the Steward's Hall was completed in December, 1870. The front building was named Callanan Hall in 1880 in honor of James Callanan, an alumnus, who at that time freed the Seminary from debt.

The name of the school was changed in 1829 from the "Seminary of the Genesee Conference" to the "Seminary of Genesee and Oneida Conference" and in 1830 it was changed from that to the "Oneida Conference Seminary." In 1868 the name was changed to "Central New York Conference Seminary" and in 1873 became "Cazenovia Seminary."

The first society organized in the Seminary was called the Oneida Conference Seminary Temperance Society, bearing date of 1830. The Lyceum, which was the first strictly literary society, was organized in 1833. The second literary society was the Delta Pi, organized in 1836, dissolved in 1843. The Phrenological Society, The Theological and Missionary Society, the Society of Inquiry and the "Les Soeurs" Society were of short duration.

Philomathesian organized in 1843, Eromathean in 1856 and Adelphian in 1866.

The Seminary had a Navy in 1875 which held regattas on the lake. Lyceum and Philo each formed a boat club and built a boat house at the outlet of the lake. A six-oared gig, or practice boat, was bought of the Cornell Navy, and two six-oared shells were added. The crews held morning and evening practice. The Commodore's full dress uniform of pale blue color, with a bib in front, counterbalanced by a bib behind, was not liked by some of the ladies as difficulty was experienced in deciding which was the front side.

The old court house is the nucleus of the group of buildings which has since sprung up around it. It is the chief cornerstone of the group, uniting Williams Hall on the east with the dormitories on the west. At the time of the purchase of the court house and of the opening of the school, there were two rooms on the lower floor and Principal Porter, with the entire school, occupied the west room. The next term, the assistant principal occupied the east room. This was provided with unpainted seats and desks. The east room soon became so crowded that several of the older students were allowed to occupy the second story. The surroundings of the school grounds were not the most enchanting. The ground where the Methodist Church now stands, down to the corner of Lincklaen and Albany streets and for several yards westward, was covered with scrub oak.

There are now thirteen buildings housing the different sections of the school. The first building or court house, ultimately, became the chapel of the larger school. On the ground floor are the laboratories and the science recitation room. Above is the chapel with its stained glass windows, given by recent graduating classes and the literary societies, and its array of portraits, many of them in oil, of illustrious alumni. In 1882, the Ledyard family, who donated the chapel organ, had it thoroughly repaired. The chapel was renovated at that same time and again in 1910.

Eddy Hall, which was repaired and refurnished in 1881, is the home of the president and the main dormitory for girls. Williams Hall contains the administrative offices, the boys' society halls, and most of the recitation rooms. In 1918 Williams Hall was made in every way modern and yet the historic features were preserved. Callanan Hall contains the parlors, the literary society rooms for the young women, the dining room and dormitories.

In 1883 General H. W. Slocum, an alumnus, gave rifles and other military equipment and for some years compulsory drill was given to the boys, under the instruction of an older student. The company was called Slocum Guards.

Water was brought from the Jackson Spring on the Nelson road in the summer of 1884. When the village system* was installed in 1890 the Seminary was also connected with it. The athletic field was first rented in 1886. An Alumni society was approved by the trustees in 1886.

The bell in the tower, which called the students to prayers and recitations for many years, was purchased from public subscriptions. This has been superseded by an electric system which is general throughout all the buildings.

The cottage, built in 1886, houses the Infirmary, with separate rooms for boys and girls and a trained nurse on one side. On the other a professor and the senior boys.

Previous to 1874 an imposing Alumni building was proposed, but it has never been built. Between the years 1887-91, three houses on Nickerson street, adjacent to the campus, were bought and removed after 1900 and the ground was made part of the campus. The gymnasium, built in 1898, is fitted with modern apparatus. It is much used, not only for gymnastic exercises, but for social gatherings, receptions and banquets. The heating plant was installed in the gymnasium in 1912. The Bible Study department organized in 1900. The Studio building, purchased in 1910, contains the studios of the teachers of violin, art, home economics and also music practice rooms. The Domestic Science department was organized in 1914. The Keppel House, bought in 1919, is used as a dormitory for several boys and one professor on the upper floor, with library and reading rooms on lower floor. The Vollmer House, purchased in 1920, was fitted up as a dormitory to accommodate twenty girls and a house mother (lady teacher). The Morse House was opened in 1921 as a home for senior girls. A house directly opposite the main buildings was purchased in 1924 for future development as the lot is a very large one. For the present it houses the Commercial or Business School, and contains an apartment occupied by the superintendent of buildings and grounds. The first floor of the Jackson House, purchased in 1925, is given over to a reception room, the studios of the piano and vocal teachers and a practice room. The upper floor is used as a dormitory for six girls and a teacher. The last building erected is the Centennial building, built in 1925. It contains a modernly equipped kitchen, small dining rooms, matron's rooms, laundry and store rooms. The second and third floors are dormitory rooms for two teachers and thirty-five boys. It is the finest building on the campus.

The Seminary is probably the oldest existing conference seminary in Methodism, founded as such, and for a century has done a work the importance of which only eternity will reveal. It has been distinguished for its strong and healthful religious influence. It has ever maintained a high

---

*The village voted in March, 1927, to purchase 30 acres of land east of the reservoir to prevent pollution of the water supply.

standing, numbering among its pupils many who have from time to time gone forth to fill the most honored stations in society. No similar school can boast of a more illustrious alumni. Eminent statesmen, theologians, educators, financiers, and many leaders in yet other fields of endeavor had their preparatory training here. It has given to the Methodist Episcopal church five Bishops.

The Centennial anniversary of the founding of Cazenovia Seminary brought to the venerable old school the largest number of alumni and visitors that have returned since the semi-centennial fifty years ago. They came in such numbers that it was difficult to find accommodations for them in the village.

On the big day of Commencement week, over six hundred persons were served at the alumni luncheon. Automobiles lined the streets about the Seminary and flags were flying all around the village. The uniform display of flags through the business section also added to the gala appearance. The crowning feature of the week's festivities was the historical pageant given in the Methodist church.

The pageant unveiled a series of pictures covering the period of the first fifty years of Cazenovia Seminary, 1924 to 1874. Efforts were made to make the scenes as historically true as possible. The prologue showed the dawn of the spirit of Cazenovia and was followed by six scenes, the first being "The Purchase of the Property"; the second, "Chapel Service Latter Part of April, 1825"; the third, "Cazenovia's Gift to Humanity," showing the various countries influenced by the missionaries; the fourth, "Civil War Chapel Scene"; fifth, "The Girl I Left Behind Me Society"; sixth, a Grand Finale, showing principals for the first fifty years and a tableaux comprised of the entire cast of seventy-two characters, while the chapel bell pealed nearby.

> "The same old bricks are in the tower,
> The bell rings to and fro,
> For the Spirit of Cazenovia is just the same,
> Dear friends, as a hundred years ago."

CULTURE

Chapter VII.

Culture

Culture, intellectual or social, is a source of enjoyment and happiness to its possessor. In whatever sphere in life a man may move, the higher the degree of his culture, the greater are the sources of his enjoyment and the better prepared is he for the discharge of any duties, private or public, that he may be called upon to perform.

Cazenovia, once called "The Newport of New York State," has been said to be a seat of wealth, culture and refinement, and these combined with its natural attractions, and eligible location, make it a favorite summer resort. It has all the alluring features which entice travellers across the ocean, for seclusion and rest. As a retreat, it is a "Mecca" to the weary one; in easy access to all main lines of traffic, it is a part of the world, yet not of it, and untrammelled by the electric car with its rush and roar which breaks the tranquility of many other summer resorts.

People prominent in official as well as social life of Washington came to spend the warm months here with ten times the pleasure and at one-tenth the cost that would be obtained and incurred at a fashionable watering place. Families from Baltimore, Philadelphia, New York and other place were counted among the visitors who made up the cottage colony. In order to take care of these people, boarding houses were established, each catering to a certain number. As time elapsed, some families built their own homes near the lake shores, while others returned to the cottages year after year. There were handsome horses and carriages, tallyhos, tandems, four-in-hands and saddle mounts, while on the lake were seen any number of boats. The evening dinner hour brought out the women in beautiful long trained gowns and the men in full dress. The children were always accompanied by maids, sometimes a colored "mammy." Daniel Webster, after visiting Cazenovia at one time remarked it was the "handsomest town he ever set his two feet in."

Today finds a few boarding houses left, a few of the "old school"; homes on the lake shore occupied by the younger generation. Motors have replaced the horses and carriages, the lake is mostly deserted except for an occasional bathing party; however interest in sailboat racing is being revived. Mild tennis with afternoon tea is indulged in at the club house while the more energetically inclined pursue the golf balls over the links. Although the town does not progress rapidly it still is an attractive place with all its natural scenery. Looking down from the hill crests upon the village, we can say with Shakespeare "How green you are, and fresh in this old world."

Grand and stately old trees line the streets on either side—and as we walk under their shadowy branches, we say—"trees shall be my books, and in their barks, my thoughts I'll character." Improved roads make the neighboring towns and cities quickly accessible. The villagers are privileged to enjoy the movies the year round; the Redpath Chautauqua each summer. In the winter, there are horse races on the lake, also picnic, skiing, coasting and skating parties. The young people attending the Seminary give a little life to the town during the dark winter months. Nearly all the town children go from grammar school to the Seminary and many are fortunate to be afforded a college education after completing the work there. Many of those not so fortunate leave town to secure employment, though at present a machine shop and diepress company, year-round industries, are giving employment to a great many.

An old scrapbook contributes the following:

"REMINISCENCES OF CAZENOVIA"

"To the Editor of the Courier:

"Reading the interesting notes on 'Summer People and Pleasures in Cazenovia,' contained in the Syracuse Standard of August 8, has brought to mind 'Sainted Memories,' and indeed,

> 'Like angel troops they come,
> As I fold my arm and ponder
> On the old, old home,
> The heart has many passages
> Through which pure feelings roam;
> But its middle aisle is sacred
> To the old, old home.'

"Twenty, twenty-five, yes, thirty years and more memory goes back to those long summer days in Cazenovia, days beautiful then as now, with a quiet and a restfulness all their own. Dear old Cazenovia; then no steamboat whistle ever pierced the air or tried the nerves with its shriek, or foul, black smoke rushed upward to make impure the clear fresh air on the 'lake of the silver perch,' beautiful Owahgena. On the quiet waters the only sound was the splashing of an oar, or sweet note of song, or ripple of laughter as the dwellers by the lake would paddle along unmolested, and at any point could anchor or pulling the boat upon a bank, quietly read or dream away the hours the whole day long. Many times and oft have we been lulled to sleep by the music of frogs, and music indeed it was, the deep bass, the tenor, even the baritone and the contralto, and speaking of this a story is called to mind: A certain clergyman, who was an early riser and who delighted in the singing of the frog, boarded at the same house with a gentleman well known to old Cazenovians, who liked to indulge in a morning nap occasionally. On a certain morning, when he had been asleep rather later than usual and came in to breakfast when the rest of the family were about through, the clergyman who had been out as usual said to him, 'My dear friend, I have been out listening to the frogs this morning and what do you suppose they said?' 'Well,' replied the gentleman whose name by the way was Guiteau, 'I'm sure I cannot tell.' 'They said,' continued the other, 'Guiteau get up, Guiteau get up.' No fashionable city life had as yet crept into this beautiful town and the 'natives' as the Standard article calls them, went about with an exclusiveness and a dignity all their own. Never gay city life could have moulded the characters of those whose homes were the center of all that was lovely, all that was beautiful and of good report. Let us look for a moment into the dear old Presbyterian church of times gone by. High up it stood on steps that were many, many times trodden by those who are now indeed saints in that 'land which is very far off,' steps where childish feet delighted to romp up and down, playing at 'catch,' 'Dickey's Land,' etc., shocking the dignity of our elders. Does not the memory of that church as it was in the old days still linger with those of us who are left? The pulpit up the long stairs where stood the sainted Leonard and Kollock of many long years ago, and later the austere but dearly beloved Doctor Barrows, a Gillette and later on our own Doctor Boardman, to whose sermons as children we listened and wondered if the big cobweb in the upper corner toward which he often pointed, had anything to do with the heaven of which he told us. With loving hands he blessed those whom he married and with tender words of comfort to the mourner he laid away our dear ones. The long galleries running way round the church, toward which as the years went on, shy glances would be cast to see the occasional seminary student who might be in one of the front seats. Down below we can well recall almost every face, as Sunday after Sunday it would be seen in the old familiar place. Sunday, too, was the busiest day in all the week, with its morning service, Sabbath school at noon, service in the afternoon with a sermon, and again in the evening. Three sermons in one day, what would pastor and people think of that nowadays. Often and often have we eaten lunch standing in order to be back in season for afternoon service, when in spite of all resolves to the contrary we sometimes would go to sleep, and not only ourselves but we well remember certain dignitaries of the church sitting back with handkerchiefs over the head to keep off the flies and sound asleep. But the Presbyterian church was not all of Cazenovia. The stone church of the Methodists stood where now it does, in different dress, its bell then called its worshippers together and the town clock then struck the hours and told us many times that we were late for chapel or recitation. Neither have we forgotten how, in an 'Upper chamber', the first services of the Episcopal church, now the prosperous St. Peters, were started. Does not memory also take us back to the 'training days,' looked forward to the whole year through? When the town would be in holiday dress and the militia, gay with gilt and feathers, would march about keeping step to the music of drum and fife, and then mass on the square where they would rest and buy ginger bread from the little stands scattered about. What days were those; how we loved the sound of that fife and drum, and with doll in arms would sit on the steps and watch the intricate maneuvering of the wonderful soldiers. Then the walks, the botanizing expeditions down the plank road past the paper mill, down past the big red mills, near which lived a dearly loved Sabbath school teacher, on to Shelter Valley, where grew and bloomed Sweet Williams and where we always found good things to eat; the drives to the springs, where congregated the fashion and gaiety of the city. Beautiful long drives around the lake, down through Pig City, where even now thought loves to dwell on the fat porkers taking solid comfort in the puddles along the streets of that city. The winter sleigh rides through the fields, over the fences and on the lake, where there was no ice cutting and no ice houses on the shore, but all was white and clear and silent. How long and sunny were the days in that olden time; how memory loves to recall them now. Beautiful and bright and gay as Cazenovia now is, it cannot be happier than when in those dear old days, we romped and roamed together, and were taught always to be courteous and dignified. Then it was said 'there never were any poor people in Cazenovia,' for how could there be when every one knew and loved his neighbor, and no one 'passed by on the other side,' or waited for the one 'good Samaritan.' Beautiful for situation is Cazenovia, beautiful now, beautiful then in its quiet and peaceful living. Many, many have been the changes, yes and improvements, but though

>'Like a wreath of scented flowerets,
>   Close intertwined each heart,
>Though time and change in concert,
>   Have blown the wreath apart.
>
>Yet sainted, sainted memories,
>   Like angel troops they come,
>When I fold my arms and ponder
>   On the old, old home.'
>   AN OLD CAZENOVIAN."

Rev. H. D. Stebbins said, "Truly, Cazenovia's children can be pardoned if they be proud of her; for beautiful as she is, her comeliness is not merely that of blue skies, rolling hills, fresh verdure and bright waters, but the better beauty of refinement, hospitality, intelligence, fairness and Christian virtue and good will."

www.ingramcontent.com/pod-product-compliance
Lightning Source LLC
Chambersburg PA
CBHW070426080426
42450CB00030B/1522